Thermo-Struck

Kim
McCosker

Thermo-Struck

Turntable Enterprises Pty Ltd
PO Box 400
Caloundra QLD 4551
ABN: 48 159 202 614

You can see more of Kim McCosker's work at:

- facebook.com/4ingredientspage
- 4 Ingredients Channel
- 4ingredients.com.au
- @4ingredients
- instagram.com/4ingredients
- @4ingredients

Photography: Stuart Quinn Photography
                    Turntable Enterprises Pty Ltd
Cover & formatting: Splitting Image
                    www.splittingimage.com.au
Image credits: P. 91 "RetroClipArt/Bigstock.com"
                    P. 98 "RetroClipArt/Bigstock.com"
                    P. 131 "RetroClipArt/Bigstock.com"
                    P. 195 "RetroClipArt/Bigstock.com"
                    P. 237 "RetroClipArt/Bigstock.com"
Cover illustrations: Tara Hale Illustration & Design
                    www.tarahale.com
Printing & Binding: Leo Paper Group,reprinted 2016
                    www.leo.com.hk
ISBN: 978-0-9805959-3-2

Foreword

When NewWave Kitchen Appliances first approached me to endorse Thermochef Natura, my initial response was, 'Do I need another electrical appliance in my kitchen?'

But I have friends who absolutely swear by its *ease* and *convenience* so out of curiosity I started playing and mixing and … *cooking!*

Within a few recipes I was what we have now come to term **'THERMO-STRUCK!'**

Who knew that one appliance did *soooo many amazing things?* One appliance whose functions result in the creamiest porridge and ice-creams. Who in five seconds creates the yummiest salads, kneads the tastiest breads and delivers incredibly warm pasta sauces that compliment mains! With extraordinary features for just one appliance, I was astounded how much I'd not only use it, but actually look forward to using it!

As the author of Australia's biggest self-published cookbook titles '4 Ingredients' I am all about saving time and money in the kitchen. I get *very* excited when I learn of recipes; kitchen tips and utensils that help me achieve either, yet still allow me to create nutritious and delicious family food.

With enthusiasm and passion, I want to share the recipes that transformed my relationship with my thermo to one of utter love and devotion. And it is my wish that through them you all become **Thermo-Struck** with *whatever* Thermo-Appliance you use too!

… *With Love* Kim

. . . I've been

Thermo-Struck!

Table of Contents

Why A Thermo?

I've always desired a personal chef in my busy home and with my thermo I've finally realised my dream, just as you will with whatever thermo appliance you are using too.

Breakfast, lunch and dinner, using fresh wholesome fruit and vegetables and good quality meats I know *EXACTLY* the ingredients I'm using to fuel the minds and bodies of my growing family.

Whether entertaining friends, whipping up nutritious meals mid-week, a quick snack or delightfully naughty dessert … Nothing is tooooo hard for my thermo!

One Appliance,
Thousands of Possibilities!

A Thermo Can

Weigh
with inbuilt
electronic scales

Blend
baby food, juices,
smoothies, soups,
crushed ice

Chop
vegetables, nuts

Grate
chocolate, cheese

Mince
meat

Mix
cakes, desserts

Whip
egg whites, cream, sauces

Milling /Grinding
seeds, spices, sugar

Knead
breads, pizza bases, pastries

Turbo boost
instant high speed

Cook
whatever is required, dry
roasting spices, temperature
control

Steam
fish, poultry and vegetables

Timer
with inbuilt electronic clock

Thermo Parts

When opening your thermo packing box, take out all the accessories and get to know them. Although they may be called something slightly different, you should easily be able to determine what they are and how they are used. Look out for the instruction manual, DVD if present, recipe book, warranty card and rating label sticker.

The accessories are as follows:
1. Main body
2. Steamer cover
3. Steaming mesh
4. Steamer
5. Steaming pot
6. Measuring cup
7. Cup lid
8. Butterfly bar
9. Blade base components
10. Blender bowl
11. Filter basket
12. Scraper
13. Scraper bracket
14. Scraper handle
15. Scraper bar

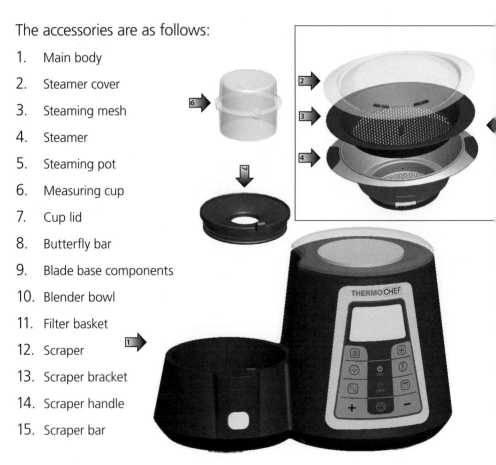

Thermo Tips

MC – Measuring Cup

MC = 100ml

100ml = 100g (when using thermo scales 100ml = 100g)

Knead – 2 minutes maximum (automatic setting)

Cook Mode – 110°C / Speed 1 (automatic setting)
When using, use a minimum 1 litre (1000g) water.

Turbo Boost – 5 seconds is the maximum amount of time this function should be used in one boost.

Electronic Scales – Can weigh up to 3kg. Can 'tare.' When you tare the balance it sets the scale to zero.

Thermo Bowl – 2L stainless steel bowl with heating system and temperature sensor. Not dishwasher safe.

Thermo Lid – Store separately from the jug to aerate.
If odours persist, simply wash, dry and dust with 2 tablespoons Bicarbonate of soda.

Butterfly Bar – Clip the lower edge of the butterfly bar onto the lower, sharper blade and turn to lock into place. Doing this prevents cutting and chopping and is great for curries and risottos.

Filter Basket – Can be used as a colander, to steam an egg, to stew meats, and is brilliant boiling / steaming light fluffy rice. Can be pulled out of the jug using the spatula handle.

Cleaning – 3 drops of dishwashing liquid + 2 cups hot water, then turbo boost for 4 seconds and if the heat function was used you may need to unlock the blades and use a steel-o pad or what you would use to clean a stainless steel saucepan.

DO NOT IMMERSE the thermo bowl in water as the electrical currents to operate it run from its base.

Thermo Wisdom

Christine Silver: **Brown Rice:**

Place in basket for 20 minutes / 100°C / Speed 1. Then added veggies and fish in steamer bowl 20 minutes / Cook Mode. Perfect!

Janelle Crofts: **Polenta:**

Follow the measurements on the back of the packet and then place the ingredients into the thermo bowl. Cook 12 minutes / 100°C / Speed 3.

Alana Fletcher: **Best Boiled Egg:**

Is a STEAMED EGG. Add 2 cups (500g) water to the bowl. Place two eggs into the filter basket. Cook 10 minutes / 100°C / Speed 1.

Amanda Hunt: **Freezing Fresh Herbs:**

Chop herbs 5 seconds / Speed 8 and then place them in an ice-cube tray with a little chicken stock and freeze. The cubes will add flavour to vegetable sautés, risottos and soups.

Michelle Evans: **Fluffy Rice:**

400g rice, 900g water. Rinse rice. Pour the water into the thermo bowl. Insert basket with rice 15 minutes / Cook Mode. Remove basket with the aid of the thermo spatula handle when cooked.

Jan Neale: **Tender Meat:**

I used to do all my casseroles and curries in the slow cooker, but my thermo is amazing. Just insert your butterfly bar to ensure it keeps its shape.

Leanne Maloni: **Sauté 1 Onion:**

Peel and quarter onion, load evenly around the blade. Turbo boost 3 seconds. Add olive oil, turbo boost 2 seconds to evenly distribute olive oil. Sauté 3 minutes / 90°C / Speed 1.

Guide to Weights & Measures

When I first started cooking with my thermo, I was so accustomed to using the basic measurements 1 cup, 1 tablespoon and 1 teaspoon that I found measuring everything into grams time consuming and, in many cases, not necessary.

So if you are like me and cook easily using a 1 cup measurement, you will find this table a FABULOUS guide to helping you use your thermo too.

TIP: When you measure dry ingredients like flour and sugar, always hold the measuring cup over the thermo bowl while you fill it up.

Product	Grams per Cup
All-Bran	70
Almond meal	110
Almonds, raw	168
Apricots, dried	160
Arborio rice	185
Banana, mashed	260
Basil pesto	260
Barley, pearl	220
BBQ sauce	280
Blueberries	150

Product	Grams per Cup
Breadcrumbs, dry	115
Breadcrumbs, fresh	60
Butter	230
Cashews, raw	160
Cheese	100
Chicken, cooked & chopped	150
Chickpeas, dried	210
Chocolate buttons	190
Cocoa powder	112
Coconut, desiccated	80

Product	Grams per Cup	Product	Grams per Cup
Cornflour	150	Pistachios, raw	120
Couscous	185	Popcorn	40
Dates, dried	170	Polenta, dried	100
Dried mixed fruit	170	Quinoa, raw	200
Flour – plain	170	Raisins	170
Flour – self-raising	170	Rasberries, frozen	130
Honey	320	Rice, raw, medium-grain	185
Icing sugar	120	Rice Bubbles	80
Jam	320	Rolled oats	100
Leek, sliced	90	Salsa	175
Macadamias, raw & whole	125	Sesame seeds	130
Marshmallows, medium-sized	96	Sour cream	250
Maple syrup	240	Sultanas	170
Mayonnaise	260	Sugar, brown	220
Milk	250	Sugar, caster	200
Natural muesli	110	Sugar, raw	200
Pine nuts, raw	160	Sugar, white	220
Parmesan, finely grated	90	Sunflower seeds	130
Passata	250	Sweet chilli sauce	320
Pasta, dried	75	Tandoori paste	225
Pasta sauce, chunky	175	Tomato paste	260
Peanuts, raw	150	Tomato sauce	280
Peanut butter	260	Walnuts, raw	120
Pecans, raw	120	Water	250
Pecans, halves raw	130	Yoghurt	250
Peas, frozen	128	Zucchini, diced	133
Peas, split green	225		

Breakfasts

Breakfast is Très Importante and with your Thermo there is no reason to skip it anymore.

Porridge, Crepes, Breakfasts on the run, ideas that are nutritious and fast!

10-Second Coconut Bread

This is a variation of the beautiful recipe as seen on the front cover of 4 Ingredients Cook 4 a Cure.

Serves 8

- 1 cup (170g) self-raising flour
- ⅔ cup (80g) desiccated coconut
- ½ cup (100g) sugar
- 270ml can coconut milk, shaken

Preheat the oven to 180°C. Line a 27 x 11cm loaf tin with baking paper. Pop all ingredients into the thermo bowl.

 10 seconds

 7

Once the batter is combined, pour it into the prepared tin, using the spatula to remove remaining batter and bake for 40 minutes or until golden and firm to touch. Remove from the oven and allow to cool on a wire rack. Serve dusted with a little icing sugar or the delicious **Rosewater Buttercream** on p. 234.

OPTIONAL: Throw in ½ cup blueberries when mixing the other ingredients together, the combination of blueberries and coconut is just heavenly.

A Breakfast on the *Run!*

Serves 1

- ½ cup (55g) natural muesli
- ¼ cup (40g) raw almonds
- 1 frozen banana, chopped
- 3 tablespoons (60g) yoghurt
- 1 cup (250g) soy milk

Pop the muesli and almonds into the thermo bowl.

  4 seconds

Add remaining ingredients.

  10 seconds

  8

A healthy breakfast high in fibre will help keep diabetes, heart disease, and stroke at bay, and can also help you achieve and maintain a healthy weight.

Apricot & Almond Porridge

This is one of my all time favourite breakfasts as no added sugar is required for a naturally sweet porridge.

Serves 4

- ½ cup (50g) rolled oats
- ½ cup (80g) raw, unsalted almonds
- 10 dried apricots
- ½ cup (125g) almond milk
- 1 cup (250g) water

Place oats, almonds and apricots into the thermo bowl.

   4 seconds

Add the liquid.

   8 minutes

   90°C

   1

Serve immediately.

Banana, Chia & Coconut Porridge

Turn your morning porridge into something delightfully special with the addition of healthy chia seeds.

Serves 2

- ⅓ cup (35g) rolled oats
- 1 tablespoon (15g) chia seeds
- 1 tablespoon (10g) moist coconut flakes
- 1 banana, quartered
- 1 teaspoon honey
- 1 cup (250g) water
- ¾ cup (180g) almond milk

Place all ingredients into the thermo bowl.

 9 minutes

 100°C

 2

Serve immediately.

Breakfast Risotto

If you have never made risotto for breakfast, you should.
IT IS DELICIOUS, and in the Thermo ~ it is EASY!

Serves 4

- 1 cup (185g) Arborio rice
- 2 teaspoons vanilla extract
- 4 tablespoons (60g) sugar
- ½ cup (85g) sultanas
- 1 litre almond milk

Insert butterfly bar into the thermo bowl and add all ingredients.

 20 minutes

 100°C

 1

Serve immediately.

TIP: A Thermo is a super machine for making dairy-free milks of
all kinds. To make your own **Almond Milk**, place 1 cup (160g)
almonds in 800g water and blend for 1 minute/speed 10.
Strain into a large bowl. For a slightly thicker milk, use 250g
almonds and 900g water. Store the strained almond milk
in a glass jar in the refrigerator and the leftover pulp in
the freezer for other recipes.

Briefcase Bircher

Serves 1

- ⅓ cup (35g) rolled oats
- 6 raw almonds
- 4 raw hazelnuts
- 1 teaspoon sultanas
- ½ apple (or ¼ apple, ¼ pear)
- 4 tablespoons (80g) yoghurt
- 1 teaspoon honey

Place the oats, almonds and hazelnuts into the thermo bowl.

   3 seconds

Pour the oat mix into a small bowl, add the sultanas and mix through yoghurt. Soak overnight in the fridge.

The next morning, place the apple and honey into the thermo bowl.

   2 seconds

   5

Stir the apple and honey through the oat mix. Spoon into a small airtight container and mix in yoghurt and sultanas. Place into briefcase with a spoon for those mornings when you dine on the run with your 'briefcase'.

Crumpets

Makes 6

- 1 tablespoon raw sugar (or white sugar)
- ¾ cup (130g) self-raising flour
- ¼ teaspoon baking powder
- 1 egg
- ⅔ cup (160g) milk

Place sugar into the thermo bowl.

 3 seconds

 9

Add remaining ingredients.

 10 seconds

 7

Using the spatula, scrape down the sides and stir the base to release any stuck flour.

 5 seconds

 4

Add a little butter to a nonstick frying pan and also grease 4 round egg rings. Over a low heat, add approx. 2 to 3 tablespoons of the batter to each egg ring and cook without turning for 6 to 8 minutes, or until the surface has dried and is full of holes. Crumpets are cooked when the bubbles stop rising to the surface. Using a long, sharp knife, run it around the inside rim to help release the crumpet. If you like the 'top toasted' remove the egg ring and flip, cooking for 20 seconds.

Lady Coconut

Serves 4

- ¾ cup (90g) moist coconut flakes
- 5 Medjool pitted dates
- ½ cup (80g) raw, unsalted almonds
- 1 tablespoon chia seeds
- 6 strawberries, washed and hulled
- 2 tablespoons (40g) blueberry yoghurt

Pop all the ingredients, except strawberries and yoghurt, into the thermo bowl.

 3 seconds

Using the spatula, push the mixture down into the blades. Add strawberries.

 1 second

Serve in a bowl or glass and dollop with blueberry yoghurt.

You Tube *4 Ingredients Channel / Date & Almond Delight (Lady Coconut)*

TIP: Chia seeds are a 'superfood' packed full of goodness. They are gluten-free and a natural source of essential fatty acids (omega 3 & 6), fibre, antioxidants, protein and amino acids – they contain all 8 essential amino acids and more. Essential minerals; calcium, zinc, iron, phosphorus, magnesium, manganese, copper, potassium and Vitamins A, B & E ... Try to incorporate them into as many things as you can!

Maple Spiced Breakfast Risotto

Serves 4

- ½ cup (90g) Arborio rice
- 1 cup (250g) water
- 2 pinches of salt
- 1 cup (250g) coconut milk
- ¼ teaspoon vanilla extract
- ½ teaspoon ground cinnamon
- ¼ teaspoon ground cardamom
- 2 tablespoons (40g) maple syrup (more to taste if desired)
- 2 teaspoons chia seeds
- 1 small banana, sliced

Add Arborio rice, water and salt to thermo bowl.

⏱ 8 minutes

🌡 100°C

✲ 1

Add remaining ingredients (except banana).

⏱ 10 minutes

🌡 100°C

✲ 1

After 6 minutes, remove the MC and add ¾ of the banana. When the risotto is soft and cooked, pour into two bowls, stud with remaining banana and ENJOY.

OPTIONAL: Drizzle with maple syrup and a sprinkling of chia seeds to serve.

Marmalade

Makes 4 cups

- 4 oranges (800g), sliced and seeds removed
- 1 cup (250g) water
- 2½ cups (550g) sugar
- ¼ cup (60g) Cointreau (optional)

Place the orange slices and water into the thermo bowl.

 10 minutes

 100°C

 1

Add the sugar and Cointreau.

 45 minutes

 100°C

 2

If the mixture starts to 'spit' remove the MC to allow steam to escape. Test the marmalade is set by scooping a little marmalade with a teaspoon and let it cool down. If it is thick and wrinkles when pushed up with the finger then it's set. Pour into sterilised jars, seal and keep in a fridge once open.

OPTIONAL: Use this to make **Marmalade Biscuits***, a retro biscuit that is really scrummy. Insert butterfly and add 110g softened butter and ½ cup (100g) caster sugar to thermo bowl; Mix 2 minutes/Speed 4. Add 1 egg; Mix 1 minute / Speed 4. Remove butterfly and scrape down sides of the bowl. Add ¾ cup (250g) marmalade and 1½ cups (255g) self-raising flour; Mix 2 minutes/Speed 4. Dollop the mixture onto baking trays and allow for spreading. Bake for 12 minutes or until slightly golden.*

Peanut 'Better'

Makes 1 cup

- 1½ cups (225g) peanuts
- ½ cup (60g) macadamia nuts

Place both nuts into the thermo bowl.

 10 seconds

 7

Use spatula to push the paste down into the blades.

 10 seconds

 7

Place in an airtight jar in the fridge.

*TIP: Make double the quantity for a lovely gluten-free **Peanut Butter Biscuits**;*
Preheat oven 180ºC. Add 1 cup (260g) peanut butter + 1 cup (220g) brown sugar
+ 1 egg + 1 teaspoon ground cinnamon and mix 30 seconds/speed 4. Scrape down
the sides of the bowl and mix again 30 seconds/speed 4. Using a tablespoon roll into
balls, place on a paper lined baking tray, press gently with a fork and bake for 10 to
12 minutes. Allow to cool completely, as they will continue to set whilst cooling.

Nutella Crepes

Makes 12

- 1 cup (250g) milk
- 1 cup (250g) water
- 1 cup (170g) plain flour
- 1 egg
- 1 teaspoon cinnamon
- 1 teaspoon nutmeg
- 1 tablespoon (15g) butter
- 4 tablespoons (80g) Nutella

Place the ingredients, except Nutella, into the thermo bowl.

 30 seconds

 5

Heat a 20cm crepe pan or small frying pan over a medium heat. Lightly grease with butter. Pour a quarter-cup of the batter into the pan and swirl to coat the entire base. Cook for 2 minutes or until golden and lacy. Flip and cook for a further 30 seconds. Transfer to a plate and repeat with the remaining batter. Then as the French do, spread with Nutella … *Bon Appétit!*

Power Porridge

Serves 4

- 1 cup (100g) rolled oats
- ¼ cup (40g) raw, unsalted almonds
- 2 tablespoons chia seeds
- 1 cup (250g) milk
- 1 cup (250g) water
- ½ cup (75g) blueberries

Place oats, almonds and chia seeds into the thermo bowl.

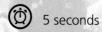 5 seconds

 8

Add the liquid.

 8 minutes

 90°C

 1

In the last minute, remove the cap from the lid and add the blueberries. Serve immediately.

OPTIONAL: Sprinkle with a teaspoon of brown sugar or a drizzle of honey. This is a great start to power you through the day.

Scrambled Eggs

Serves 2

- 1 tablespoon (15g) butter
- ⅓ cup (80g) milk
- 4 eggs
- 1 tablespoon chopped parsley

Add butter to the thermo bowl and melt.

 1 minute

 50°C

 1

Swirl the melted butter over the bottom and around sides of the thermo bowl (use a pastry brush), including the blades. Add milk and eggs and parsley.

 10 seconds

 4

 12 minutes

 90°C

 2

OPTIONAL: Serve over a toasted piece of ciabatta or Turkish bread with a dollop of the delicious **Quick-Fire Tomato Jam** *p. 111.*

Smoothie Bowls

Serves 2

- 1½ cups (200g) frozen mixed berries
- 1½ bananas (use the remaining half to garnish)
- 2 tablespoons (30g) peanut butter (or almond butter)
- ⅔ cup (160g) water
- 12 ice cubes

Place all ingredients into the thermo bowl.

 30 seconds

 8

When thick and creamy, pour into a bowl and top with sliced banana.

OPTIONAL: Sprinkle with any of the following toppings; Granola, moist coconut flakes, blueberries, strawberries, grapes, kiwi, goji berries, chia seeds, pomegranate seeds, almonds or pumpkin seeds.

Smoothies

Smoothies are a great snack, high in vitamins and minerals and are **especially** good on mornings when time escapes us as a quick, nutritious breakfast on the run.

B Fresh

Serves 2

- 2 kiwi fruit, peeled and cut in half
- 2 apples, cored and quartered
- 200g seedless white grapes
- 6 cubes of ice

Place all ingredients into the thermo bowl.

 20 seconds

 10

Pour into two glasses to serve.

BBG (blueberry, banana, green tea)

Serves 1

- 1 green tea bag
- ¼ cup (60g) boiling water
- 1 tablespoon (15g) honey
- 1½ cups (225g) blueberries
- 1 banana
- ¾ cup (180g) soya milk

Steep the tea bag in the boiling water for 2 minutes. Place all ingredients into the thermo bowl.

 30 seconds

 9

Pour into a glass to serve.

Berry Berry Smooooooth

Serves 2

- 200g strawberries, washed and hulled
- ½ cup (70g) frozen raspberries
- ¾ cup (180g) rice milk
- ¼ cup (30g) natural muesli

Place the ingredients into the thermo bowl.

 30 seconds

 9

Pour into glasses and serve.

Blueberry Blast

Serves 2

- 1 cup (130g) frozen blueberries
- 2 frozen bananas, chopped
- 2 tablespoons (30g) cashew butter
- 1 tablespoon (20g) honey

Place the ingredients into the thermo bowl.

 30 seconds

 8

Serve immediately over a little crushed ice.

"Date Your Banana" Shake

Serves 2

- 2 cups (500g) almond milk
- 4 Medjool pitted dates
- 2 medium bananas, peeled and chopped
- ¼ teaspoon nutmeg
- ¼ teaspoon cinnamon
- 10 ice cubes

Pop all ingredients into the thermo bowl.

 30 seconds

 8

Serve immediately.

Fitness First

Serves 2

- 1 mango
- 4 kiwi fruit
- 250g chopped pineapple
- 6 fresh mint leaves
- 6 ice cubes

Peel and slice the fruit. Place the fruit, mint and ice into the thermo bowl.

 30 seconds

 9

Pour into glasses and serve.

Flu-Buster

Serves 2

- 3 oranges, peeled, cut and seeds removed
- 12 strawberries, washed and hulled
- 200g paw paw (papaya), peeled and deseeded
- 1 frozen banana

Place the ingredients into the thermo bowl.

 30 seconds

 9

Serve in two tall glasses.

Thermo-Struck Smoothies

Green Goddess

Serves 4

- ½ Lebanese cucumber, sliced
- 2 large handfuls spinach
- 250g chopped pineapple
- 1 frozen banana, chopped
- 1 tablespoon (15g) honey
- ½ lime, juiced
- 2 cups (500g) water
- 8 ice cubes

Place all ingredients into the thermo bowl.

 30 seconds

 10

Serve when nice and smooth … and *green!*

You Tube *4 Ingredients Channel / Healthy Smoothie (Green Goddess)*

Strawberry Oatmeal Smoothie

Serves 2

- 1 cup (250g) almond milk
- ½ cup (50g) rolled oats
- 1 frozen banana, chopped
- 12 frozen strawberries
- 1 tablespoon (20g) honey

Place all ingredients into the thermo bowl.

 40 seconds

 8

Blend until nice and smooth. Pour into glasses and serve.

Virgin Pink Mojito

Serves 2

- 4 cups seedless watermelon, cut into chunks
- 1 tablespoon (20g) honey
- 8 mint leaves
- ½ lime, juiced
- 10 ice cubes

Pop all ingredients into the thermo bowl.

 30 seconds

 8

Pour into two beautiful glasses and garnish with sprigs of fresh mint.

Snacks

Snacks can offer health
benefits, aim to eat your snack
about halfway between meals
to keep energy levels consistent
and your metabolism ticking.

Be Thermo-Healthy!

30-Second (no bake) Chocolate Brownies

Makes 16

- 1 cup (170g) almond meal
- ½ cup (60g) cocoa powder
- 2 tablespoons brown sugar
- 2 cups (340g) pitted dates
- 2½ tablespoons (40g) coconut oil
- ⅓ cup (40g) walnuts
- ¼ cup (30g) moist coconut flakes

Line an 18cm square cake tin with baking paper. Place almond meal, cocoa powder and sugar into the thermo bowl.

 10 seconds

 4

Add the dates and coconut oil.

 15 seconds

 8

Add walnuts.

 5 seconds

 8

Using the spatula, scrape the mixture into the prepared tin then using your hands bring the dough together, pressing gently across the base of the tin. Level the surface, then sprinkle with the coconut, pressing it lightly into the surface. Cover with cling wrap, and chill for at least 2 hours before slicing to serve.

Apricot Balls

Makes approx. 20

- 200g dried apricots
- ½ cup condensed milk
- 1 cup (120g) moist coconut flakes
- ¾ cup (90g) desiccated coconut

Into the thermo bowl, place the dried apricots.

 5 seconds

 5

Add condensed milk and moist coconut flakes.

 10 seconds

 5

When combined, roll the mixture into 2cm wide balls, roll in coconut, cover and refrigerate until required.

TIP: These delicious balls are perfect as a sweet treat in school lunchboxes so make double and freeze. They are also perfect to have on hand when someone drops in unexpectedly.

Almond Crusted Pâté Parcels

Makes 16

Filling

- ¼ cup (40g) raw, unsalted almonds
- ½ onion, peeled and halved
- 2 slices bacon, rind removed and chopped
- 6 button mushrooms, sliced
- 2 tablespoons (30g) olive oil
- 200g pâté of choice

Base

- 6 sheets filo pastry
- ½ cup (115g) butter, melted

Place the almonds into the thermo bowl.

 3 seconds

Remove and set aside. Place the bacon and onion into the thermo bowl.

 4 seconds

Add the mushrooms and olive oil.

 4 minutes

 90°C

 2

Add the pâté.

 30 seconds

 3

Unroll the filo sheets on a flat surface. Take one sheet and lay it out on a clean work surface and brush with butter, repeat two more times, so you have a stack of three buttered sheets.

Cut the stack into eight, 5cm-wide strips. Place one tablespoon of pâté at the end of each strip. Fold the end of the strip over the filling so that it forms a triangle.

Continue folding the strip in triangles until a small, triangular stuffed parcel results. Brush with butter and sprinkle with crushed almonds, place onto a paper lined baking tray. Repeat until the filling is all used. Bake in a preheated oven 12 to 15 minutes or until golden brown. Serve warm.

Apricot & Date Bars

Makes 12 bars *or* 36 squares

- 300g dried apricots
- ⅓ cup (50g) pitted dates
- 1 cup (120g) desiccated coconut
- ¼ cup (30g) flaked almonds (optional)

Line a small 27 x 11cm loaf tin with baking paper. Place all ingredients into the thermo bowl.

 10 seconds

 7

Scrape down the sides of the thermo bowl, pushing mixture onto blades.

 20 seconds

 8

Using the spatula, spoon the mixture into prepared tin. Smooth out using the back of a spoon (it may need to be damp if sticking to the slice). Refrigerate for 1 hour. Remove from tin. Slice into 12 bar shapes or 36 pieces. Roll in desiccated coconut. Refrigerate in an airtight container for up to 10 days.

TIP: If the mixture is too dry, process a little longer or add an extra date or two.

Chocolate PB Balls

Makes 18

- ¾ cup (120g) raw almonds
- 1 tablespoon (8g) cacao powder (you could also use cocoa powder)
- 14 pitted dates (or 10 if Medjool*)
- 2 tablespoons peanut butter
- 2 tablespoons (40g) agave syrup (honey or rice malt syrup could also be used)

Into the thermo bowl, place the almonds.

 4 seconds

Add remaining ingredients.

 10 seconds

 6

Scrape down the sides of the thermo bowl, pushing mixture onto blades.

 10 seconds

 6

If the mixture is too dry, add a little more agave syrup and pulse to mix through. If it is still too dry add a tablespoon of water, and pulse again. The mixture should be a little sticky. Using a teaspoon, roll into balls. Refrigerate in an airtight container for up to 10 days.

If using fresh Medjool dates you will probably find that you will only need a tiny amount of agave syrup – or none at all!

Chocolate Slice

Makes 12

- 1 cup (100g) peanuts
- 250g Scotch Finger biscuits
- 375g milk chocolate melts
- ½ cup (115g) butter, cubed

Place the peanuts into the thermo bowl.

 10 seconds

 6

Using the spatula, push the peanuts down onto the blade. Add the biscuits.

 8 seconds

 4

Using the spatula, remove the mixture and set aside. Add the chocolate.

 10 seconds

 8

Add the butter.

 4 minutes

 37°C

 2

Using the spatula pour the buttery chocolate into the biscuit mixture and mix thoroughly. Spoon the mixture into a paper-lined 28 x 18cm baking tray and refrigerate for at least 1 hour or until set. Allow the slice to warm slightly, then using a hot knife, cut to serve.

Choc-Toffee Truffles

Makes 20

- 140g packet Werther's Originals hard toffees
- 200g milk chocolate, chopped
- ⅓ cup (80g) thickened cream
- ½ teaspoon vanilla extract
- ¼ cup (30g) cocoa powder

Place the toffees into the thermo bowl.

 5 seconds

 8

Add the chocolate, cream and vanilla.

 4 minutes

 37°C

 1

With 1 minute remaining, remove the MC and add the toffee dust. Use the spatula to mix the mixture together, then refrigerate in the thermo bowl for 30 minutes. Line a baking tray with baking paper and using a teaspoon, roll the mixture into balls. Sift the cocoa onto a shallow dish, and roll the balls lightly to coat. Place on the prepared tray and refrigerate for another 30 minutes or until firm.

COOKIE AllsortS

Makes 40

- ¾ cup (165g) sugar
- 400g butter, cut into tenths
- 400g can condensed milk
- 5 cups (850g) self-raising flour
- 40 Licorice Allsorts

Preheat the oven to 180°C. Line 2 baking trays with baking paper. Place sugar into the thermo bowl.

 5 seconds

 7

Add butter.

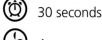 30 seconds

 4

Scrape down the sides of the bowl. Add condensed milk and flour.

 40 seconds

 3

or until combined. Chill for 10 minutes in the refrigerator. Take a heaped tablespoon of dough. Press a Licorice Allsort into it. Work the dough around the licorice, or add a little more dough to completely cover it entirely. Place on the prepared tray, about 3cm. Press gently with a fork. Bake for 15 minutes or until just golden. Cool completely before storing in an airtight container.

TIP: This recipe lends itself so well to many add-ins. Think choc chips, dried fruits, chopped nuts, sprinkles, flavoured sugars. It also freezes well wrapped in glad wrap.

Energy Bars

Makes 12

- 1 cup (170g) pitted dates
- ¾ cup (200g) crunchy peanut butter
- ½ cup (60g) moist coconut flakes
- 3 tablespoons (24g) cocoa powder

Place all the ingredients into the thermo bowl.

 8 seconds

 6

Using the spatula, push the mixture down into the blades.

 8 seconds

 4

Spoon the mixture into a paper-lined 20 x 10cm loaf tin. Smooth the top with the spatula (or back of a spoon). Refrigerate for at least 1 hour. Cut into bars. Keep in the refrigerator in an airtight container.

*TIP: To make your own delicious, nutritious **Peanut Butter** (Better!) see p. 28. To make it crunchy simply reduce the mixing time by half or until you reach the desired consistency.*

Fruit Roll Ups

Makes 16 Strips

- 900g strawberries, washed and hulled
- 1½ tablespoons sugar
- ½ teaspoon vanilla extract

Preheat oven to 75°C. Line two baking trays with baking paper. Place all ingredients into the thermo bowl.

 25 seconds

 9

Pour the mixture over the prepared trays, half on each. Smooth the mixture evenly, with a knife, across the trays. Place into the oven for 2 hours or until no longer soft in the middle and only slightly tacky. Remove from the oven and sit for 10 minutes before slicing or cutting into strips. Store in an air-tight container.

TIP: If still moist, sit in a sunny spot to dry completely.

Halva Bites

Makes 24

- ½ cup (80g) raw hazelnuts
- ¼ cup (35g) hulled sunflower seeds
- ½ cup (60g) coconut, finely shredded
- ¼ cup (80g) honey
- ¼ cup (80g) tahini
- Pinch of sea salt

Into the thermo place hazelnuts and sunflower seeds.

 4 seconds

Add coconut, honey and tahini, season with a generous pinch of sea salt.

 10 seconds

 6

Scrape down the sides of the thermo bowl, pushing the mixture onto the blades.

 10 seconds

 6

Using a teaspoon, and with damp hands, roll the mixture into balls.

TIP: For the best flavour, allow the balls to set for 24 hours before eating. Store in a tightly sealed container in the refrigerator where they will last for up to 2 weeks.

I'm SO HAPPY Slice

OMG … THIS IS SOOOO GOOD!

Makes 8

- 2 cups (200g) rolled oats
- ½ cup (130g) natural crunchy peanut butter
- ½ cup (160g) honey (use agave for a vegan option)
- ¼ cup (50g) chocolate chips (use dairy-free if needed)

Preheat oven to 180°C. Line a 27 x 11cm loaf tin with baking paper.

Place the first three all ingredients into the thermo bowl.

 10 seconds

 5

Scrape the mixture into a bowl. Add the chocolate chips and stir to combine. Press the mixture firmly into the prepared tin. Bake for 20 minutes or until the edges just start browning. Cool for 10 minutes, and cut into bars. Store in a cool dry place for up to a week (though, I guarantee it won't last this long!)

OPTIONAL: I have made this delicious slice substituting raisins for chocolate chips, dried apricots and white chocolate chips, raspberries and white chocolate chips ~ options are endless.

You Tube *4 Ingredients Channel / I'm SO HAPPY Slice*

Key Lime Balls

These are TherMOST delicious balls ever!

Makes 16

- ½ cup (85g) pitted dates
- ¼ cup (40g) raw, unsalted almonds
- ½ lime, juice and 1 teaspoon zest
- 3 tablespoons (20g) desiccated coconut

Place all ingredients into the thermo bowl.

 5 seconds

 8

Using the spatula, push the mixture down into the blades. Use Turbo Boost for 1 to 2 seconds for a finer consistency. Using a teaspoon, and damp hands, roll a generous amount of mixture into a ball and place on a plate. When all are rolled, cover with cling film and chill for at least 20 to 30 minutes.

TIP: These freeze beautifully.

Lemon Slice

Serves 10

Base

- 250g packet sweet biscuits (Arrowroot, Nice etc)
- 1 cup (120g) desiccated coconut
- 1 teaspoon lemon zest
- ½ cup (150g) condensed milk
- ½ cup (115g) butter, softened

Place the biscuits into the thermo bowl.

 10 seconds

 8

Pour the crumbs into a large mixing bowl and add to them the coconut and zest. Place the butter and condensed milk into the thermo bowl.

 2 minutes

 37°C

 2

Using the spatula, add this mixture to crushed biscuits and mix well.
Press into a paper-lined 28 x 18cm baking tray and refrigerate for one hour.

Lemon Icing

- 1¾ cups (210g) icing sugar
- 1 teaspoon butter
- 3 tablespoons (45g) lemon juice
- 2 tablespoons (12g) desiccated coconut

Place icing sugar, butter and lemon juice into the thermo bowl.

 30 seconds

 4

Use the spatula to mix the icing together then spread across the slice and sprinkle with coconut. Cut into squares to serve.

Mango Magic

Serves 8

- 4 ripe mangoes, peeled and roughly chopped
- 2 limes, juiced
- 6 mint leaves
- 24 ice cubes
- 2 cups (500g) water

Place all ingredients into the thermo bowl.

 30 seconds

 8

*OPTIONAL: For a delicious **Mango Daiquiri** add ½ cup of Bacardi Rum and ½ cup of vodka. Pour into martini glasses and serve garnished with fresh mint leaves. These make a perfect pre-dinner refreshment when entertaining and especially when served with the delicious **Thai Chicken Balls** on page 73 ~ a delightful combination to wow your guests.*

Pesto Prawns

Makes 12

- 75g Parmesan, cubed
- 50g coriander leaves
- 1 clove garlic, chopped
- ¼ cup (40g) cashews, toasted
- ¼ cup (60g) olive oil
- 200g cooked prawns, peeled, tail on
- ¼ iceberg lettuce, finely shredded
- 1 tablespoon (15g) olive oil
- 1 tablespoon (15g) fresh lemon juice

Place Parmesan into the thermo bowl.

 5 seconds

 8

Add the coriander, garlic, cashews and oil.

 4 times

Using the spatula stir well then set aside until required. Combine the lettuce, oil and lemon juice, season to taste and toss to coat. Top with the prawns and serve with pesto.

TIP: If you have leftover pesto refrigerate and serve with baked potatoes, on toast, pasta and atop steamed fish or chicken.

Rum Balls

My husband's logic … "Come on, they've got Weetbix in them, they must be good for me??"

Makes 48

- 12 Weetbix
- ¼ cup (60g) rum *(I used Bundaberg … Is there another??)*
- 400g can condensed milk
- ¾ cup (90g) desiccated coconut

Place the Weetbix into the thermo bowl.

 4 seconds

 8

Add remaining ingredients, except ¼ cup (40g) of coconut, place that onto a large plate.

 10 seconds

 2

Using a teaspoon, roll the mixture into balls, then into the coconut to coat. Place on a plate and repeat until all the mixture is gone. Refrigerate until ready to serve.

TIP: These freeze beautifully.

Salted Raisin Pecan Balls

Makes 30

- 2 cups (240g) raw pecans
- 1 cup (170g) raisins – or – currants
- ¼ cup (80g) agave nectar
- ¼ teaspoon sea salt

Place all ingredients into the thermo bowl and season with sea salt.

 10 seconds

 6

Scrape down the sides of the thermo bowl, pushing mixture onto blades.

 10 seconds

 6

Using a teaspoon, roll the mixture into balls. Store in a tightly sealed container in the refrigerator where they will last for up to two weeks.

TIP: These freeze beautifully.

Semi-Dried Tomato Pesto

Makes 1½ cups

- 1 clove garlic, quartered
- 150g semi-dried tomatoes
- 150g roasted, marinated capsicums, drained
- 200g feta cheese
- 2 tablespoons (40g) sweet chilli sauce

Place the garlic into the thermo bowl.

 3 seconds

Add the remaining ingredients, and season with cracked pepper.

 20 seconds

 6

Scrape down the sides of the bowl, pushing the mixture onto the blades.

 10 seconds

 4

Serve with fresh veggie sticks and Melba toast.

*OPTIONAL: For another really tasty **Rocket & Walnut Pesto** simply place 60g rocket + 1 cup firmly packed fresh basil + ½ cup roasted walnuts + 2 cloves garlic, crushed + 1 teaspoon lemon zest + ⅓ cup Parmesan cheese + 1 tablespoon olive oil into thermo bowl. Turbo boost for 3 seconds. Using the spatula, push mixture down onto blades and add 2 tablespoons olive oil. Mix 20 seconds, speed 6. Add 1 more tablespoon olive oil and blend till the mixture is smooth. Season to taste.*

Sugarless Banana Ice-cream

Serves 2

- 2 frozen bananas, chopped
- ¼ cup (65g) coconut milk, shaken
- 1 teaspoon vanilla extract

Combine all ingredients into the thermo bowl.

 4 seconds

Using the spatula, scrape down the sides of the bowl.

 20 seconds

 8

Pour the soft serve into a freezer safe container. Cover and freeze for at least 2 hours to create a thick, creamy sugarless ice-cream.

*TIP: With the leftover coconut milk, make a yummy 4 Ingredient **Thai Green Curry** for dinner. Fry off 1 tbsp. Thai green curry paste, add chicken pieces and sauté stirring regularly for 3 to 4 minutes. Add leftover coconut cream and green beans, cover and simmer for 10 minutes. Serve over fluffy jasmine rice, garnished with fresh coriander leaves.*

Sesame & Honey Bars

Makes 12

- 1 cup (130g) sesame seeds
- 1 cup (100g) rolled oats
- ½ cup (160g) honey
- ½ cup (115g) butter, softened

Preheat oven 180°C. Add the sesame seeds and oatmeal to the thermo bowl.

 4 seconds

Add the honey and butter.

 4 minutes

 60°C

 4

Use the spatula to scrape the mixture into a paper-lined 28 x 18cm baking tray. Bake for 20 minutes, or until golden brown. Cool slightly before slicing to serve.

Thai Chicken Balls

Makes 6

- 250g chicken, breast or thigh, roughly chopped
- 1 Spanish onion, peeled and quartered
- ½ cup (80g) roasted, salted cashews
- 3 tablespoons (45g) Gourmet Garden Thai Blend
- 1 tablespoon lime zest
- ¼ cup (60g) olive oil

Place the chicken into the thermo bowl.

 10 seconds

 7

Remove and set aside. Place the onion and cashews into the thermo bowl.

 5 seconds

 7

Scrape down the sides. Add chicken mince, Thai blend and lime zest.

 20 seconds

 7

Roll one tablespoon of the mixture into a ball. Over medium heat, heat the oil in a nonstick frying pan, gently fry the balls in batches, stirring for 4 to 6 minutes or until cooked and golden brown.

*OPTIONAL: Serve with sweet chilli sauce to dip or our **Quick Dipping Sauce** on page 123.*

White Chocolate & Macadamia Nut Cookies

*This yummy recipe came from Debbie Wuoti,
the lovely lady behind TM-essentials, accessories for your
Thermo-Appliance* **www.tm-essentials.com.au**.

Makes 30

- 100g raw macadamias
- 125g white chocolate buttons
- 4 tablespoons (60g) sugar
- 1 cup (170g) self-raising flour
- 100g soft butter, chopped
- 1 egg

Preheat oven to 180°C and line baking tray with baking paper. Place the macadamias into the thermo bowl.

 3 seconds

 4

Pour into a bowl, add white chocolate buttons and set aside. Place the sugar and 1 tablespoon of flour into the thermo bowl.

 4 seconds

Insert butterfly and add butter.

 1 minute

 3

Add egg.

 1 minute

 3

Remove butterfly and add flour, macadamias and white chocolate buttons.

 30 seconds

 3

or until well combined, I did push it all down half way through. Form into small balls and place onto tray at least 5cm apart. Bake in the oven for 10 minutes or until firm on the bottom.

Dips

Served solo as part of a tapas platter, or in a trio you can't go wrong with a tasty dip. They are simple to make, and with fresh ingredients take literally **seconds to whip** up in your Thermo.

Creamy Jalapeño Dip

Serves 6

- 1 cup (250) sour cream
- 1 cup (260g) mayonnaise
- 2½ tablespoons Dry Ranch Style Seasoning (see next page)
- ½ cup pickled jalapeños, drained
- ½ cup fresh coriander, washed and dried
- 2 tablespoons fresh lime juice

Place all ingredients into the thermo bowl and season with cracked pepper.

 20 seconds

 8

Scrape down the sides of the bowl, pushing the mixture onto the blades.

 10 seconds

 6

Serve with fresh veggie sticks and Melba toast.

TIP: Pickled jalapeños are available in the Mexican aisle of your supermarket.

Dry Ranch Style Seasoning

*This yummy seasoning is HUGE in the States, sold
pre-packaged like our French Onion Soup, it is just
delicious used in rissoles or mixed with breadcrumbs as
crumbing for pan fried chicken, fish or steak and in the
Creamy Jalapeño Dip on previous page.*

Makes approximately 5 tablespoons (¼ cup)

- 2 tablespoons dried parsley
- 3 teaspoons ground black pepper
- 2 teaspoons sea salt
- 2½ teaspoons garlic powder
- 1¼ teaspoons onion powder
- ¾ teaspoon dried thyme

Place all the ingredients into the thermo bowl.

  5 seconds (twice)

Store in a zip lock bag. To make a **Ranch Dressing**, 1½ tablespoons of
Seasoning with 1 cup mayonnaise and 1 cup buttermilk. For a yummy Ranch
Dip, mix 1½ tablespoons of seasoning with 1¾ cups sour cream and ¼ cup
of buttermilk.

Hummus

Serves 6

- 1 garlic clove
- 400g can chickpeas, drained
- ¼ cup (60g) fresh lemon juice
- 2 tablespoons (45g) tahini
- 2 tablespoons (30g) water
- 1 teaspoon ground cumin
- ½ teaspoon ground coriander

Place the garlic into the thermo bowl.

 5 seconds

 7

Scrape down the sides using the spatula. Add the remaining ingredients.

 1 minute

 50°C

 4

SERVING SUGGESTIONS: Warm hummus on crunchy crostini topped with a splay of fresh parsley, or dollop a generous tablespoon onto a plate, fan with avocado and top with a poached egg ... Thermo-Licious!

Feta Dip with Spiced Pita Crisps

Serves 8

- 200g feta
- ¼ cup (60g) olive oil
- 1 garlic clove, chopped
- ¼ cup (60g) milk

Place the feta, oil and garlic into the thermo bowl.

 1 minute

 4

Half way through remove MC and steadily add the milk until a smooth paste forms. Using the spatula scrape the dip into a serving bowl and refrigerate until ready to serve with these scrumptious pita crisps …

SPICED PITA CRISPS

- 2 large wholemeal pita breads
- 1 tablespoon (15g) olive oil
- 1 teaspoon ground cumin seeds
- 1 teaspoon ground coriander seeds
- 1 teaspoon sesame seeds
- 8 black peppercorns
- ½ teaspoon paprika

Meanwhile split the pita breads in half, brush both sides with oil and lay on a baking tray. Into the thermo bowl place cumin, coriander, sesame seeds, peppercorns and paprika. Roast 1 minute / 100°C / speed 1. Mill 30 seconds / Speed 8. Sprinkle over the oiled pita breads.

"In a flash" SALSA

Serves 6

- 2 cans (400g each) diced tomatoes, drained
- 1 jalapeño, seeded (1 jalapeño results in a medium salsa)
- 1 small onion, peeled and quartered
- 1 teaspoon garlic salt
- ½ teaspoon sugar
- 2 teaspoons cumin
- 2 teaspoons lime juice

Place all ingredients into the thermo bowl and season with cracked pepper.

 30 seconds

 8

My family love this on their Burritos, Tacos and Nachos. It's also really nice mixed with diced avocado and fresh coriander and served with Corn Chips as a Dip.

Salmon & Parsley Log

Serves 8

- 1 cup curly parsley
- 250g cream cheese, cut into quarters
- 35g pkt salt reduced French Onion Soup mix
- 220g can salmon, drained and flaked
- 1 tablespoon (15ml) lemon juice

Into the thermo bowl, place the parsley.

 4 seconds

 7

Set aside. Into the thermo, add remaining ingredients and season with cracked pepper.

 5 seconds

 5

Scrape down the sides of the bowl.

 10 seconds

 5

When combined, use the spatula to scrape the mixture onto a sheet of wax paper, then roll, shaping it into a log. Chill for at least 30 minutes. Roll the chilled log into the freshly chopped parsley and onto a serving platter with a side of crackers and veggie sticks.

Salmon Pâté

Serves 6

- 1 spring onion
- 50g sliced smoked salmon
- 125g cream cheese
- ¼ cup (60g) sour cream
- ½ to 1 teaspoon horseradish
- ½ lemon, juiced

Cut the spring onion into about 3 pieces, reserving the top for garnish. Place it into the thermo bowl.

 4 seconds

 8

Scrape down and add smoked salmon.

 5 seconds

 5

Again scrape down the sides and add all remaining ingredients.

 15 seconds

 4

Serve in a bowl garnished with remaining spring onion or a pretty 'scallion flower.'

> TIP: To make a 'scallion flower' cut the remaining stalk into 5cm pieces. With a paring knife, start 2cm from the bottom of the first side and cut two slits, forming 4 tendrils. Do the same with the other side. Place the stalk in a bowl of cold, icy water for 10 minutes. Repeat with 3 or 4 other stalks. To vary, shorten the stalk to 3cm and create the tendrils on just one side. These are really pretty as garnish for fish, chicken, curries, salads and pâté.

Strawberries & Cream Dip

Makes 1½ cups

- 250g light cream cheese, softened
- ½ cup (125g) Greek yogurt
- ½ cup (160g) strawberry jam

Into the thermo bowl, place the cream cheese.

 12 seconds

 6

Add the yoghurt and strawberry jam. Scrape down the sides of the bowl, pushing the cream cheese onto the blades.

 10 seconds

 4

The dip should be nice and smooth (if not mix again: 10 seconds, speed 4). Cover and chill for at least one hour or until ready to serve.

TIP: Serve this with fresh-cut chunks of seasonal fruit; rockmelon, honeydew, pineapple, apple and whole strawberries and thin slices of freshly sliced crunchy baguette … They ALL work!

Tex Mex Dip

Serves 8 to 10

- 420g can refried beans
- 3 ripe avocados
- ½ cup (130g) mayonnaise
- 1 tablespoon lemon juice
- ⅔ cup (200g) sour cream
- ½ packet (20g) taco seasoning mix
- 1 cup (100g) grated cheddar cheese
- 2 spring onions, finely chopped
- 1 small vine ripened tomato, diced

Into a round 22cm serving dish, spread the refried beans. Into the thermo bowl, place avocados (discard skin and seed), mayonnaise, and lemon juice.

 15 seconds

 4

Using the spatula, scrape the mixture from the bowl and spread over bean dip. Quickly wash and dry the bowl. Combine the sour cream and taco seasoning.

 10 seconds

 4

Spread over first two layers. Sprinkle with cheese, then spring onions, then tomato. Cover loosely and refrigerate overnight to "marry" the flavours.

TIP: Serve with tortilla chips and stand back ... it's a STAMPEDE!

Warm Cheese Fondue

Serves 8

- 200g cheddar cheese, cubed
- 2 tablespoons (30g) butter
- 1 teaspoon ground cumin
- ¾ cup (180g) sour cream

Place cheese into the thermo bowl.

 5 seconds

 8

Set aside. Add the butter and cumin.

 20 seconds

 60°C

 1

Add sour cream and cheese.

 5 minutes

 80°C

 2

Pour the dip into a serving bowl and serve with a platter of freshly sliced, crusty baguette or vegetable crudités to dip.

Breads and Doughs

Thermos have reintroduced the wonders of home baked bread to our lives, and we are loving it ... Hope you do to!

Beautiful Bread

Makes 1 loaf

- 350g lukewarm water
- 2 teaspoons salt
- 2 tablespoons (30g) sugar
- 600g bakers flour
- 14g dry yeast

Place water, salt and sugar into the thermo bowl.

 20 seconds

 2

Add the flour and yeast in that order.

 2 minutes

The dough should come together, using the spatula, spoon the dough into a lightly oiled large bowl. Cover with cling film and set aside in a warm place (I placed mine on a sunny bench) for at least 30 minutes or until it has doubled in size.

Preheat oven 220°C. Turn the dough out onto a paper-lined baking tray. Glaze with milk, sprinkle with sea salt and bake for 30 to 40 minutes.

You**Tube** *4 Ingredients Channel / Beautiful Bread*

TIPS: I want to share a couple of really simple, useful tips I learnt when starting to bake bread.

- *A Thermo only kneads for 2 minutes, it's an automatic timer when the knead function is selected*
- *Always use lukewarm water*
- *Never allow the salt and yeast to come into contact … Salt deactivates the yeast*
- *Always allow the dough to rise in a warm 22–25°C place (even on cooler days).*

Pizza Dough

Makes 4 bases

- 220g lukewarm water
- 50g olive oil
- 7g dry yeast
- 500g bakers flour
- 1 teaspoon salt

Place the water, oil and yeast into the thermo bowl.

 5 seconds

 3

Add the flour and the salt.

 2 minutes

Using the spatula, spoon the dough into a lightly oiled large bowl and cover with cling film. Leave to rest in a warm place for at least 30 minutes or until it has doubled in size. Divide dough in half (for two large pizzas, or into four if making smaller ones) and place on a clean, floured surface. Using a floured rolling pin roll the dough into pizza bases and add your family's favourite toppings. Bake in a preheated 220°C oven for about for 20 minutes.

TIP: Pop a small ball of dough in a glass full of water. When the ball bobs, the dough is well leavened or ready for baking.

Herb & Garlic Foccacia

Makes 1

- 1¼ cups (300g) lukewarm water
- 2 teaspoons olive oil
- 7g dry yeast
- 500g bakers flour
- 1½ teaspoons salt
- 1 teaspoon mixed herbs
- 1 teaspoon Gourmet Garden Chunky Garlic

Place the water, oil and yeast into the thermo bowl.

 5 seconds

 3

Add the flour, salt, herbs and garlic.

 2 minutes

Turn the dough out into a large lightly oiled bowl and cover it with cling film. Leave to rest in a warm place, I used my windowsill, for 30 minutes or until it has doubled in size. Preheat oven 210°C. Place the dough onto a paper lined baking tray, and roll it out into a long 2cm thick rectangle. Lightly brush with olive oil and sprinkle with a variety of toppings; herbs, garlic, sea salt, cracked pepper or grated Parmesan or pecorino cheese and bake for 15 minutes.

TIP: My eldest boy loves this sliced and lightly toasted as a BLT.

Scrolls

- 1¼ cup (300g) lukewarm water
- 2 teaspoons yeast
- 1½ tablespoons (20g) vegetable oil
- 3 cups (500g) bakers flour
- 2 teaspoons sea salt

Add all ingredients into the thermo bowl.

 5 seconds

 5

Scrape down the sides of the thermo bowl, pushing mixture onto blades.

 30 seconds

 1

Empty from thermo bowl and shape into a smooth ball (also known as 'a mushroom shape' all tucked under itself). Wrap in a bread mat (www.tm_essentials.com.au) or cover with glad wrap and let prove for 30 minutes. Divide dough in two and roll out onto a clean, floured surface. Spread with any number of …

DELICIOUS FILLINGS

Vegemite and grated cheese
Pizza paste, cheese, ham and pineapple
Basil pesto and grated Parmesan
Nestle Caramel Top 'n' Fill, sprinkled with sultanas

Preheat oven to 210°C. Spread the filling over the dough, leaving a 1cm strip along one long side. Roll up like a Swiss roll. Cut each into 12 rounds, taking care not to squash the roll. Lay scrolls onto a paper lined baking tray, about 3cm apart. Bake for 15 minutes, or until golden brown.

Yummy Bread Rolls

Makes 16

- 2 tablespoons (30g) plain flour
- 2 tablespoons (30g) sugar
- 1⅓ cups (330g) buttermilk
- 350g bakers flour
- 1¼ tablespoon (20g) butter, softened
- 7g dry yeast

Place the plain flour, sugar and ½ cup (125g) buttermilk into the thermo bowl.

 3 minutes

 80°C

 3

Cool for 5 minutes. Add remaining ingredients (except yeast).

 10 seconds

 6

Add yeast.

 2 minutes

Turn the dough out into a lightly oiled bowl. Cover with cling film and leave sit in a warm place (best between 20 to 25°C) for 30 minutes or until it has doubled in size. Slice the dough into 16 squares and place them side by side on a paper-lined baking tray. Bake in an unheated 180°C oven for 20 minutes.

Zucchini Bread

Serves 10

- 250g zucchini, quartered
- 1 small onion, peeled and chopped
- 2 cups (340g) self-raising flour
- ⅓ cup (80g) vegetable oil
- 4 eggs
- ½ cup grated Parmesan cheese
- ½ cup chopped herbs

Preheat oven to 180°C. Line a 27 x 11cm loaf tin with baking paper. Into the thermo bowl, pop the zucchini and onion.

 5 seconds

 7

Add remaining ingredients and season with sea salt and cracked pepper.

 10 seconds

4

Scrape down the sides of the bowl.

10 seconds

4

When combined, pour / scrape the mixture into the loaf tin. Bake for 50 to 60 minutes or until an inserted skewer removes clean. Cool before slicing. Serve with a dollop of the delicious **Quick-Fire Tomato Jam** p. 111, a bowl of your favourite veggie soup or as an accompaniment to any BBQ.

Lunches

SALADS

Best Beetroot Salad Ever

Serves 4

- 2 beetroots, peeled and quartered
- 1 carrot, quartered
- ½ Spanish onion, peeled and cut in half
- ½ cup chopped coriander leaves
- 1 lemon, juiced
- 2 tablespoons (30g) extra virgin olive oil

Place all the ingredients into the thermo bowl and season with sea salt and pepper.

 4 times

This salad cemented the wonderful relationship I have with my Thermo.

Kale & Strawberry Salad

Serves 6

- 200g kale, stalks removed
- 250g strawberry, hulled and sliced
- ¾ cup(100g) sunflower seeds
- ⅓ cup(80g) balsamic vinegar
- ⅔ cup (160g)extra virgin olive oil
- 1 tablespoon (15g) water
- 2 teaspoons caster sugar
- 1 tablespoon freshly chopped chives

Add kale leaves to thermo bowl.

 4 seconds

 8

Remove to salad bowl and sprinkle with strawberries and sunflower seeds. Place remaining ingredients into the thermo bowl.

 5 seconds

 8

Drizzle over the salad and toss gently to coat. Serve immediately.

I love this salad as it creates the illusion I'm a kitchen Goddess, a genius in all things culinary when really it's my Thermo!

Kim Chi

*Is a traditional Korean dish and one I enjoyed when I ate at the **amazing** Kind Living Cafe, Maleny, QLD.*

Serves 4

- ¼ head (450g) cabbage, sliced
- 1 carrot, sliced
- ½ red capsicum, chopped
- 1 onion, peeled and quartered
- 1cm piece fresh ginger, peeled
- 2 tablespoons (30g) apple cider vinegar
- 2 teaspoons honey
- 1 teaspoon sea salt

Place half the cabbage into the thermo bowl.

 10 seconds

 Speed 4

Set aside into a large salad bowl. Add the remainder cabbage, carrot, capsicum and onion.

 10 seconds

 Speed 4

Add to the cabbage and mix well. Into the thermo bowl, add the ginger, apple cider, honey and sea salt.

 15 seconds

 Speed 2

Drizzle over the salad, toss to combine and serve.

SERVING SUGGESTION: This is yummy as a side dish for most BBQ or grilled meat, fish or seafood and actually improves with age. If you store it in a jar in the fridge it can last up to one month.

Oriental Salad

Serves 6

- 1 bunch coriander leaves
- 2cm piece fresh ginger, peeled
- 100g bok choy, chopped
- 1 Chinese cabbage (remove hard base and discard), chopped
- 1 red capsicum
- ½ cup (60g) cashews

Place the coriander and ginger into the thermo bowl.

 3 seconds

 6

Add remaining 4 ingredients.

 5 seconds

 4

Transfer to a serving bowl and serve drizzled with this tasty dressing...

ORIENTAL SALAD DRESSING

Makes 1 cup

- 1 clove garlic
- 2cm piece fresh ginger, peeled
- ½ cup fresh coriander
- 4 tablespoons (60g) tamari soy sauce
- 2 tablespoons (30g) sesame oil
- ⅓ cup (80g) white wine vinegar
- 2 tablespoons (30g) lime juice

Place the garlic, ginger and coriander into the thermo bowl, chop 5 seconds / speed 6. Add remaining 4 ingredients, mix 5 seconds / speed 3.

Yummy Chickpea & Lime Salad

Serves 6

- 300g can chickpeas, drained
- ½ cup fresh, chopped coriander leaves
- 1 small chilli, deseeded and chopped
- ½ Spanish onion, peeled and chopped
- ½ Lebanese cucumber, chopped
- 2 teaspoons pink salt flakes
- 1 lime, zest and juiced
- 3 tablespoons (45g) extra virgin olive oil
- 2 avocados, peeled and cubed
- 100g English spinach

Place all the ingredients into the thermo bowl, except the avocados and spinach.

 3 seconds

 8

Lay the spinach onto a serving platter, sprinkle with avocado and drizzle with chickpea mixture.

Waldorf Salad

Serves 4

- 2 red apples, cored and chopped
- 2 green apples, cored and chopped
- ¾ cup (125g) raisins
- ½ cup (60g) walnuts
- ⅓ cup (80g) whole egg mayonnaise
- 1 teaspoon lemon juice

Place all the ingredients into the thermo bowl.

 3 seconds

 5

Did you know ...This salad is almost 120 years old?

It was first created between 1893 and 1896 at the Waldorf Hotel in New York City.

DRESSINGS, MARINADES & SAUCES

Caramelised Balsamic Vinegar

- ⅔ cup (180g) balsamic vinegar
- ½ cup (110g) brown sugar

Place the two ingredients into the thermo bowl.

 18 minutes

 100°C

 1

Pour the reduction into a jar. Set aside uncovered as it will thicken as it cools. Rinse the thermo immediately with hot, soapy water.

OPTIONAL SEASONINGS: 1 to 2 garlic cloves cut in half, sprig fresh rosemary, black pepper, 1 tablespoon port wine, orange zest.

SERVING SUGGESTIONS: Drizzle over pizza, or make a delicious salad dressing over rocket, sliced pear and soft blue cheese. Drizzle over a slice of sharp cheddar on fresh sourdough. Serve over a scoop of creamy vanilla ice-cream and fresh strawberries.

Dukkah

Makes 1 cup

- 100g macadamia nuts
- 50g sesame seeds
- 30g cumin seeds
- 25g coriander seeds
- 1 teaspoon salt
- ½ teaspoon black peppercorns
- 1 teaspoon dried thyme

Place the nuts and seeds into the thermo bowl to dry roast.

 6 minutes

 100°C

 1

Remove the lid and cool for 10 minutes. Add the remaining ingredients.

 3 seconds

This will form a coarse powder. Store leftovers in an airtight container in the refrigerator.

SERVING SUGGESTIONS: Serve with freshly sliced Turkish bread and extra virgin olive oil for dipping or lightly oil a skinless salmon fillet, coat with Dukkah and pan-fry or bake.

Quince Paste

Makes 4 cups

- 500g quince, peeled, seeds removed, roughly chopped
- 1 lemon, peel from ½ lemon, plus juice
- 2½ cups (550g) sugar

Place the ingredients into the thermo bowl.

 30 seconds

 7

 30 minutes

 100°C

 5

Allow to cool, store in an airtight container.

SERVING SUGGESTION: Cut the top layer of skin from a wheel of Camembert, keeping it to replace later. Sprinkle the top with fresh thyme and garlic. Replace the lid. Wrap in foil and place on a hotplate or BBQ for 5 minutes, or until warmed through. Alternatively, cook in the oven for 10 minutes. Transfer the cheese to a serving board and serve with quince paste, flatbread, nuts and dried fruit ... Thermo-Mazing!

Ranch Dressing

Makes 2 cups

- 1 cup (260g) whole-egg mayonnaise
- 1 cup (250g) sour cream
- 2 tablespoons (30g) fresh lemon juice
- 1 teaspoon fresh, chopped dill
- 1 teaspoon garlic powder

Place all ingredients into the thermo bowl.

 30 seconds

 6

SERVING SUGGESTION: This is really nice mixed through pasta salad, blended with egg yolks then spooned back into the egg cases or as a side to bacon and eggs in the morning.

Raspberry Balsamic Reduction

Makes 1 cup

- ⅔ cup (160g) balsamic vinegar
- 2 tablespoons (30g) honey
- ¼ cup (40g) raspberries
- Pinch of sea salt flakes

Place all the ingredients into the thermo bowl.

 10 minutes

 2

Serve as is, or pour through a sieve to remove raspberry seeds.

SERVING SUGGESTIONS: Vibrant and colourful this vinaigrette is great to serve on a nutty or fruity salad.

Watermelon & Raspberry Vinaigrette

Makes 1½ cups

- 1 cup cubed, seeded watermelon
- ½ cup (75g) raspberries (fresh or frozen)
- 2 tablespoons (30g) honey
- 1 tablespoon (15g) white vinegar

Add the watermelon and raspberries to the thermo bowl.

 5 seconds

 7

Add the honey and vinegar.

 2 times

Serve immediately, or store in the refrigerator until ready to serve, and shake before using.

Quick-Fire Tomato Jam

Makes 1 cup

- 1 Spanish onion, peeled and quartered
- 1 tablespoon (15g) olive oil
- ⅓ cup (85g) tomato paste
- ¼ cup (60g) water
- ¼ cup (55g) brown sugar
- 1 tablespoon (15g) white wine vinegar

Place the onion into the thermo bowl, loading evenly around the blade.

  4 seconds

Add olive oil.

  3 minutes

  90°C

  1

Add the remaining 4 ingredients.

  5 minutes

  100°C

  4

This is just amazing with just about anything, but I particularly like it served with **Cheesy Frittata** p. 175 and **Veggie Rissoles** p. 189.

ALL OTHERS

Cheese & Bacon COB LOAF

*A delicious creamy COB LOAF is just perfect for
a pre-lunch or dinner gathering, especially this one.
Every time I make it, I am asked for the recipe.*

Serves 8

- 1 cob loaf
- 250g rindless bacon, chopped
- 1 onion, peeled and quartered
- 1 tablespoon butter
- 250g cream cheese
- 300g cream
- 2 cups (200g) grated mozzarella
- 1 cup (100g) grated cheddar cheese
- 1 cup English Spinach, chopped

Cut the top off the cob loaf and pull the soft bread out. Preheat oven 180°C.
Place the top and stuffing aside. Into the thermo bowl, place bacon and onion.

 5 seconds

 5

Scrape down the sides and add butter.

🕐 4 minutes

🌡 100°C

✳ 1

Add cream cheese, cream and grated cheeses. Season with cracked pepper.

6 minutes

 100°C

 1

Half way through, remove MC and add spinach. Fill the cob loaf with the mixture. Place bread lid on and wrap in foil. Bake for 45 minutes. Remove foil, add bread pieces and bake for another 10 minutes, or until nice and crisp. To serve, place on a heat resistant platter with crispy bread pieces around the outside to use as dippers.

Chicken, Leek & Bacon Pies

Makes 4

- 1 leek (350g), washed and roughly chopped
- 2 rindless bacon rashers, roughly chopped
- 1 tablespoon (15g) butter
- 420g can condensed cream of chicken soup
- 3 cups leftover BBQ chicken, chopped coarsely
- 1 sheet puff pastry, quartered

Into the thermo bowl, add the leek and bacon.

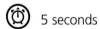 5 seconds

 5

Scrape down the sides and add butter.

 4 minutes

 100°C

 1

Insert butterfly. Add chicken soup and chicken. Season with cracked pepper.

 6 minutes

 100°C

 1

Set aside to cool, and for the flavours to develop, for 10 minutes. Preheat oven 180°C. Divide the mixture among 4 (250ml) ovenproof ramekins. Top each with a pastry quarter, tucking the edges into the inside of the ramekin. Cut two air vents into the lid of each. Bake for 20 minutes or until the pastry is puffed and golden.

OPTIONAL: Add some peas and corn to the mixture for a complete meal!

Curried Lentil Stew

Serves 8

- 1 onion, peeled and quartered
- 2 parsnips, peeled and quartered
- 2 Granny Smith apples, quartered
- 2 cups dried green lentils, rinsed
- 1 litre vegetable stock
- 2 teaspoons curry powder
- 200g cabbage, sliced into long, thin shreds

Into the thermo bowl, place onion, parsnip, apple.

 5 seconds

 1

Scrape the mixture from the blades. Add remaining ingredients (except cabbage) and season with cracked pepper.

 10 minutes

 100°C

 1

Add cabbage.

 12 minutes

 100°C

 1

Stand for 10 minutes, or until the lentils are tender. Serve over fluffy jasmine rice, with a dollop of natural yoghurt and fresh coriander leaves.

Dairy-Free Carbonara Sauce

Serves 8

- 1 large onion, peeled and halved
- 2 cloves garlic
- 2 slices of bacon
- 2 tablespoons (30g) olive oil
- 200g mushrooms, sliced
- 60g English spinach
- 2 tablespoons cornflour (dissolved in ¼ cup of almond milk)
- 2 cups (500g) almond milk (using ¼ cup for the above)
- 1 teaspoon tamari soy sauce
- 2 teaspoons vegetable stock

Place the onion, garlic and bacon into the thermo bowl.

⏲ 5 seconds

✦ 7

Scrape down the sides and add the oil.

⏲ 4 minutes

🌡 90°C

✦ 2

Add mushrooms.

⏲ 3 seconds

✦ 3

 2 minutes

⏚ 100°C

⊕ 2

Add remaining 5 ingredients, and season.

⏚ 7 minutes

⏚ 90°C

⊕ 2

Sauce should be 'thickish' to serve. Check the seasonings, and serve over rice or pasta.

WOW ... I'll never make Carbonara any other way!

Falafels

Makes 8

- ½ Spanish onion, peeled and halved
- 2 cloves garlic
- 400g can chickpeas, drained
- 2 tablespoons fresh parsley
- ½ teaspoon chilli flakes
- 2 tablespoons breadcrumbs
- 2 tablespoons (30g) plain flour
- 1 teaspoon cumin

Preheat oven to 180°C and line a baking tray with baking paper. Place all the ingredients into the thermo bowl and season.

 5 times

 20 seconds

 4

With wet hands, shape the mixture into golf size balls. Transfer to the baking tray and spray lightly with olive oil. Bake for 40 to 45 minutes, turning half way through.

*SERVING SUGGESTIONS: Falafels are delish served in a pita bread with **Hummus** p. 80 and salad, or as a main drizzled with a nice, **Homemade Tomato Sugo** p. 178 and salad.*

Fish Cakes

Makes 8

- 2 spring onions, quartered
- ⅓ cup fresh coriander
- 1cm piece fresh ginger, peeled
- 750g fresh fish fillets, chopped
- 1½ tablespoons red curry paste
- ½ cup (85g) plain flour
- ¼ cup (60g) olive oil

Add spring onions, coriander and ginger to the thermo bowl.

 5 seconds

 5

Add the fish and curry paste.

 4 seconds

Scrape down the sides.

 10 seconds

 2

Mix with the spatula, then using wet hands, shape the mixture into 8 even-sized cakes, roll in flour and chill in the fridge for 30 minutes. Heat the oil in a large nonstick frying pan and gently fry the cakes for 4 minutes each side or until golden and cooked through.

Sausage Rolls

Makes 20

- ½ cup cheddar cheese, cubed
- 1 slice multigrain bread, broken (great way to use up stale bread)
- 2 slices bacon, rind removed and roughly chopped
- ½ onion, roughly chopped
- 1 carrot, chopped
- 1 apple, cored and quartered
- ½ cup fresh parsley leaves
- 300g chicken mince (or lean beef)
- 2 tablespoon smoked BBQ sauce
- 2 sheets puff pastry, thawed

Preheat oven to 180°C and line 2 trays with baking paper. Place cheese and bread into the thermo bowl.

 6 seconds

 8

Set aside into a large bowl. Place the bacon and onion into the thermo bowl.

 4 seconds

Add carrot, apple and parsley to the thermo bowl.

 5 seconds

 8

Add the mince, BBQ sauce and season with sea salt and cracked pepper. Add the bread and bacon mixture.

 20 seconds

 4

Cut the pastry sheets in half. Roughly take a quarter of the filling and shape it into a log along the centre of each piece of pastry. Roll up to enclose the filling, and cut into 5 or 6 pieces. Place on trays, seam side down. Bake for 25 minutes or until golden.

TIP:
- *Brush with milk and sprinkle with sesame seeds for a golden finish.*
- *To mince your own meat: 400g batches, dice partially frozen meat 10 seconds / Speed 7*
- *To make your own puff pastry: 150g plain flour, 150g cold butter – diced, 75g chilled water, pinch of salt. Mix 15 seconds / Speed 6. Mix 10 seconds / Speed 2. Refrigerate for 30 minutes. Roll out as you would puff pastry.*

Spinach & Salmon Loaf

Serves 6

- 50g Parmesan cheese, cubed
- 415g can salmon in brine, drained
- 100g spinach, stalks removed
- 3 eggs
- 1 cob of corn, (or 1 small tin, drained)
- 1 tablespoon lemon juice
- ½ cup (90g) cooked rice
- 1 tomato

Preheat oven 180°C. Place the Parmesan into the thermo bowl.

 4 seconds

 8

Add all remaining ingredients except the tomato.

 15 seconds

 5

Use a spatula to pour the mixture into a 20 x 10cm paper-lined loaf tin. Garnish with sliced tomato and season with sea salt and pepper. Bake for 45 minutes or until golden. Cool and slice.

Steamed Dim Sims

Serve 4

- 1 litre water
- 1 cup (185g) basmati rice, rinsed
- 50g broccolini
- 2 bunches bok choy, washed
- ¼ cup (40g) cashews
- 660g Prawn and Vegetable Dim Sims

Place the water into the thermo bowl and insert the rice basket with the rice in it. Place the veggies in the steamer basket, first the broccolini, then the bok choy and cashews. Insert the black mesh tray, add the prawn and vegetables dim sims before the lid.

   15 minutes

Drizzle with this super easy sauce – *Thermo-Mazing!*

QUICK DIPPING SAUCE

- 2 tablespoons sweet chilli sauce
- 1½ tablespoon lime juice
- 1 tablespoon fish sauce

Meanwhile, to make the dipping sauce, combine the 3 ingredients in a small bowl. Whisk together and serve.

Sweet Corn Fritters
~ served with "Must Have Guacamole"

Makes 8

- 2 spring onions, trimmed and roughly chopped
- 2 tablespoons (30g) butter
- 3 fresh corn cobs, kernels only, removed from cob
- ¾ cup (130g) plain flour
- ⅓ cup (80g) milk
- 1 large egg
- 1 tablespoon sweet chilli sauce
- 1 tablespoon fresh coriander

Into the thermo bowl, place spring onions.

 3 seconds

 5

Scrape down the sides and add 1 tablespoon of butter.

 4 minutes

 100°C

 2

Add everything else (except remaining butter) and season with sea salt and cracked pepper.

 10 seconds

 4

Into a large nonstick frying pan, melt a little of the butter. Once hot, fry spoonfuls of the mixture for about 2 minutes each side or until golden and crisp on each side. Serve with a salsa or a quick salad of red capsicum, spring onions, tomatoes and cucumber or this …

OPTIONAL: A dollop of my "Must Have Guacamole" from **4 Ingredients Diabetes**. *Cube an avocado, finely chop half a Spanish onion, a small vine-ripened tomato and 2 tablespoons of freshly chopped coriander. Mix gently to combine. Season with sea salt and cracked pepper.*

Tuna Slice

Serves 6

- 1 small onion, peeled and quartered
- 100g cheddar cheese, cubed
- 100g Savoury biscuits
- 415g can tuna in brine, drained
- 3 eggs
- 1 cup (250g) milk
- 1 teaspoon lemon zest

Preheat oven 180°C. Place the onion, cheese and biscuits into the thermo bowl.

 8 seconds

 8

Scrape down the sides. Add remaining ingredients and season to taste.

 1 minute

 2

Pour into a paper-lined 28 x 18cm baking tray and bake for 30 to 35 minutes or until golden and cooked through.

Vegetable Flan

Serves 6

- 70g cheese, gruyère or Swiss
- 2 tablespoons fresh parsley, chopped
- 1 onion, peeled and quartered
- 1 tomato, quartered, seeds discarded
- 200g cream
- pinch of paprika
- 2 tablespoons (35g) cornflour
- 4 eggs
- 2 zucchinis, cut into 2cm-wide discs

Preheat oven 160°C. Place the cheese and parsley into the thermo bowl.

 5 seconds

 8

Remove and set aside. Add the onions.

 5 seconds

 7

Add all remaining ingredients, including cheese and parsley.

 15 seconds

 3

Pour into a baking paper-lined 20cm flan / quiche dish and season the lid well with sea salt and cracked pepper. Bake for 40 to 45 minutes or until golden and cooked. Cool to serve.

*OPTIONAL: Serve with a crisp garden salad drizzled with a little **Caramelized Balsamic Vinegar** p. 106 or sweet chilli sauce.*

Walnut, Bacon & Rosemary Sauce

Serves 4

- 70g Parmesan cheese, cubed
- ½ cup (55g) roasted walnuts
- 2 cloves garlic
- 2 tablespoons chopped rosemary leaves
- 3 tablespoons butter
- 4 slices bacon, rindless cut into thin strips
- 250g Philadelphia Cream for cooking

Add the Parmesan, walnuts, garlic and rosemary into the thermo bowl.

 4 seconds

 8

Add butter and bacon.

 3 minutes

 90°C

 1

Add cream.

 4 minutes

 100°C

 1

Serve this scrumptious sauce with your favourite pasta.

Thermo-Star!

Zucchini & Ricotta Fritters

Serves 6

- 1 zucchini, quartered
- 2 tablespoons fresh coriander leaves
- 2 tablespoons freshly chopped chives
- 2 eggs
- 160g ricotta
- ¾ cup (140g) plain flour
- 2 tablespoons (30g) olive oil
- ¼ cup (80g) sweet chilli sauce

Place zucchini, coriander and chives into the thermo bowl.

 5 seconds

 7

Add eggs and ricotta.

 30 seconds

 6

Add flour and season to taste.

 20 seconds

 6

Heat the oil in a nonstick frying pan and place heaped tablespoons of the mixture into the frying pan. Cook for 1 minute each side or until golden brown. Drain on absorbent paper and serve drizzled with sweet chilli sauce …

Mains

A Thermo really comes into its own making no-stir Risottos, Curries, a divine Cheesy Frittata with a delectable Tomato Jam, Steamed Chicken and Cashews and so much more all made effortlessly and with minimal clean-up after the cook-up!

SOUPS

Chicken & Corn Soup

Serves 4

- 1 skinless chicken breast fillet
- 1 spring onion
- 1 litre chicken stock
- 420g can creamed corn
- 1 tablespoon (15g) tamari soy sauce
- 1 egg, beaten

Cut the chicken breast into pieces, cut the spring onion into quarters and place into the thermo bowl. Add the stock and season with cracked pepper.

 5 minutes

🌡 100°C

⚙ 1

Add creamed corn and soy sauce.

⏱ 7 minutes

🌡 100°C

⚙ 1

Add the egg.

⏱ 2 minutes

🌡 100°C

⚙ 2

Season to taste and serve hot. This recipe is undeniably a *Thermo-Star!*

Cream of Mushroom Soup

Serves 4

- 500g mushrooms, halved
- 1 brown onion, peeled and quartered
- 2 cloves garlic, peeled
- 2 tablespoons (30g) butter
- 2 tablespoons (30g) sherry
- 1 teaspoon thyme
- 2 cups (500g) chicken stock
- 4 tablespoons (60g) sour cream

Place the mushrooms, onion and garlic into the thermo bowl.

⏱ 4 seconds

✛ 7

Using the spatula, scrape down the sides, then add the butter.

⏱ 4 minutes

🌡 90°C

✛ 1

Add sherry, thyme and stock.

⏱ 10 minutes

🌡 100°C

✛ 1

Cool for 5 minutes and blend for 20 seconds / speed 7 for a smoother consistency. Stir in the cream, then season with sea salt and pepper and enjoy!

Dreamy Carrot Soup

A delightfully light, gently spicy soup that when my friend
Annie first made me, made me close my eyes and murmur.

Serves 4

- 10 carrots, top 'n' tailed and chopped
- 1 Spanish onion, peeled and chopped
- ¼ teaspoon curry powder
- 2cm piece fresh ginger, peeled
- 2 cups (500g) vegetable stock
- ½ cup (60g) raw cashews
- Pinch of sea salt

Place carrots and onion into the thermo bowl.

 5 seconds

 7

Add remaining ingredients and season with cracked pepper.

 15 minutes

 100°C

 1

Cool for 10 minutes.

 30 seconds

 8

Season to taste.

Healthy Chickpea Soup

Serves 4

- 1 onion, quartered
- 2 slices bacon
- 1 tablespoon (15g) olive oil
- 1 zucchini, sliced
- 300g can chickpeas, drained
- 2 cups (500g) chicken stock

Place the onion and bacon into the thermo bowl.

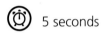 5 seconds

 7

Add the olive oil.

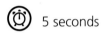 3 minutes

 90°C

 1

Add remaining ingredients.

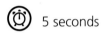 10 minutes

 70°C

 2

Cool for 5 minutes and blend for 20 seconds / speed 7 for a smoother consistency.

Mexican Mole Soup

Serves 4

- 1 tablespoon (15g) butter
- 500g chicken thighs, chopped
- 2 cups (500g) water
- 800g can crushed tomatoes
- 35g packet Taco seasoning
- 300g can corn
- 420g can red kidney beans, rinsed and drained

Into the thermo bowl, add butter.

 20 seconds

 100°C

 1

Add chicken and season with cracked pepper.

 5 minutes

 100°C

 1

Add remaining ingredients.

 12 minutes

 100°C

 1

OPTIONAL: Serve sprinkled with freshly torn coriander leaves. Add a little chilli, I would use ½ tablespoon Gourmet Garden Mild Chilli or any kind of chilli flakes.

Pea & Coconut Soup

Serves 4

- 2 spring onions, sliced
- 2cm piece fresh ginger, peeled
- ¼ cup (60g) water
- 2 x 400g cans coconut milk
- 500g green peas

Place the spring onions and ginger into the thermo bowl.

 4 seconds

 7

Add water, coconut milk and peas.

 10 minutes

 100°C

 4

Cool for 5 minutes and blend for 20 seconds / speed 7 for a smoother consistency. Season to taste then serve.

Potato & Leek Soup

Serves 4

- 2 leeks, white part only, washed and roughly chopped
- 4 tablespoons (60g) butter
- 4 potatoes, peeled and diced
- 1 litre chicken stock

Place the leek into the thermo bowl.

 10 seconds

 7

Add the butter.

 3 minutes

 90°C

 2

Add the potatoes and stock.

 15 minutes

 100°C

 2

Cool for 5 minutes and blend for 20 seconds / speed 7 for a smoother consistency.

TIP: **Leek Chips** *are a simple thing, but make a big impression. Slice desired amount of the discarded leek into 4cm lengths, then slice those into thin strips lengthwise. Heat ½ cup oil in a small frying pan and fry, stirring for 30 seconds or until the leeks just start to brown. Using a slotted spoon, gently remove the leek chips, shaking off excess oil, and transfer to absorbent paper. Serve sprinkle over the soup or as an appetizer with sea salt.*

Pumpkin Soup

Serves 6

- 1 onion, peeled then quartered
- 1 tablespoon (15g) butter
- 700g pumpkin, chopped and peeled
- 3 cups (750g) chicken stock

Into the thermo bowl, place the onion.

 5 seconds

 7

Add the butter.

 3 minutes

 90°C

 1

Add the pumpkin.

 15 seconds

 7

Add the stock and season with cracked pepper.

 20 minutes

 100°C

 4

Cool for 5 minutes and blend for 20 seconds / speed 7 for a smoother consistency. Top with a dollop of natural yoghurt or sour cream and a sprinkle of **Dukkah** p. 107.

Red Curry Cauliflower Soup

Serves 4

- 2 tablespoons Red Curry paste
- ½ (500g) head cauliflower, chopped
- 2 potatoes (200g each), peeled and quartered
- 2½ cups (625g) vegetable stock
- 1 tablespoon lime juice

Into the thermo bowl, place curry paste.

 2 minutes

 100°C

 1

Add cauliflower, potatoes and stock.

 10 minutes

 100°C

 3

Cool 10 minutes.

 5 seconds

Add lime juice.

 20 seconds

 2

Season to taste.

Tomato & Lentil Soup

Serves 4

- 2 celery stalks, trimmed and roughly chopped
- 420g can condensed cream of tomato soup
- 1 tablespoon (15g) olive oil
- 2 cups (500g) vegetable stock
- 400g can brown lentils, drained
- 2 tablespoons chopped parsley to garnish

Into the thermo bowl, place celery.

 4 seconds

 7

Add oil and season with cracked pepper.

 3 minutes

 100°C

 1

Add tomato soup, stock and lentils.

 10 minutes

 100°C

 1

Cool for 10 minutes. Spoon into serving bowls and sprinkle with chopped parsley.

Veggie Soup

Serves 4

- 600g pumpkin, peeled and chopped
- 1 onion, peeled and chopped
- 1 garlic clove, crushed
- 1 large carrot, chopped
- 3 sticks celery, chopped
- ¼ teaspoon chilli flakes (also yummy with Chipotle Flakes)
- 2 cups (500g) chicken stock
- Basil to garnish

Into the thermo bowl, place pumpkin, onion and garlic.

⏱ 6 seconds

✛ 7

Add carrot and celery.

⏱ 15 seconds

✛ 7

Add the stock and chilli flakes.

⏱ 10 minutes

🌡 100°C

✛ 1

Cool for 15 minutes.

⏱ 30 seconds

✛ 5

Or until nice and smooth. Garnish with basil to serve.

CHICKEN, MEAT & SEAFOOD

Beef Curry

Serves 6

- 1 onion, peeled and quartered
- 2cm piece fresh ginger, peeled
- 2 cloves fresh garlic
- 3 tablespoons (45g) olive oil
- 1 kg chuck steak, cut into 3cm cubes
- 400g can diced tomatoes (or condensed tomato soup)
- 3 medium potatoes, washed and cubed
- 2 tablespoons (40g) Korma paste
- ¾ cup (185g) water
- ½ cup (70g) peas

Place onion, ginger and garlic into the thermo bowl.

 3 seconds

Add olive oil.

 3 minutes

 90°C

 2

Add remaining ingredients, except peas, and season.

 25 minutes

 100°C

 1

With 2 minutes remaining, remove MC and add the peas, replace MC.

Beef Stroganoff

Serves 6

- 1 onion, peeled and quartered
- 2 tablespoons (30g) butter
- 500g rump steak, cut into thick slices across the grain
- 45g packet Stroganoff seasoning
- ¾ cup (185g) water
- 120g mushrooms, halved
- 125g cream cheese

Place onion into the thermo bowl.

 5 seconds

 7

Add butter.

 9 minutes

 90°C

 2

Add remaining ingredients, except mushrooms and cream cheese.

 20 minutes

 100°C

 1

Half way through, remove MC and add the mushrooms and cream cheese. Serve with steamed green beans and mashed potato, rice or pasta to soak up the delicious sauce.

Chicken & Sweet Onion Jam

Serves 4

- 5 Spanish onions, peeled & quartered
- 1 tablespoon (15g) olive oil
- ½ teaspoon salt
- 1 cup (250g) dry sherry
- 1 cup (250g) port
- 50g raisins
- Cracked black pepper
- 120g broccolini
- 480g chicken breast, sliced and seasoned

Place onions into the thermo bowl.

 5 seconds

 7

Scrape down. Add the oil and salt.

 4 minutes

 90°C

 1

Add the sherry, port, raisins and pepper. Place the steaming pot on top of the thermo bowl and add the broccolini. Place the seasoned chicken in the black mesh tray on a sheet of baking paper and cover.

 30 minutes

Remove the steamer and set aside. Stir the onion jam and pour approximately a quarter cup onto each of the four serving plates. Lay the chicken on top of the jam and the broccolini beside it.

Chicken, Spinach & Parmesan Meatballs

Makes 24

- 50g Parmesan, quartered
- 3 slices multigrain bread
- 10 stems of fresh parsley
- 100g English spinach
- 250g minced chicken
- 2 tablespoons cream cheese
- 1 teaspoon lemon zest
- 1 teaspoon butter

Place Parmesan and bread into the thermo bowl.

🕐 10 seconds

✛ 8

Set aside. Into the thermo bowl, place the parsley.

🕐 5 seconds

✛ 7

Add spinach.

🕐 2 seconds

✛ 7

Add remaining ingredients.

🕐 20 seconds

✛ 3

Roll into balls and lightly fry in a nonstick frying pan.

Creamy Garlic Chicken

Serves 4

- 125g Parmesan cheese, cubed
- 3 cloves garlic, peeled
- ½ cup torn fresh flat-leaf parsley
- 2 tablespoons (30g) olive oil
- 500g chicken thighs, cubed
- 250g Philadelphia Cream for cooking

Place the Parmesan into the thermo bowl.

  5 seconds

  8

Set aside. Add garlic and parsley.

  3 seconds

  8

Scrape down the sides with the spatula. Add the oil and the chicken.

  15 minutes

  100°C

  1

Add the cream and grated Parmesan cheese, season to taste.

  5 minutes

  100°C

  1

SERVING SUGGESTION: Fettucini, spaghetti or pappardelle.

Curried Fish with Coconut Rice

Serves 4

- 400g can coconut milk
- 1 cup (250g) water
- 1 cup (185g) jasmine rice
- 4 x fresh white fish fillets (approx. 150g each), skinless
- 300g jar Korma curry sauce
- ½ cup (70g) frozen peas, thawed
- 2 tablespoons (30g) raw cashews

Add coconut milk and water to the thermo bowl. Insert the filter basket with rice in it. Lock the stainless steel steamer tray into place. Onto the black mesh tray place 4 squares of alfoil. Place the fish onto each of the squares and cover with a third of a cup of Korma. Lift the edges to form a bowl and trap in the sauce. Dot the cashews around the fish. Secure with the lid.

 20 minutes

With just 5 minutes remaining, lift the lid and add the peas. Remove the steaming bowl, but keep intact to lock in the heat. Use the handle of your spatula to remove the bowl of rice. Divide evenly among 4 plates, top with the fish, drizzle with the yummy sauce and serve with the peas and cashews.

Lamb & Eggplant Ragu

Serves 4

- 1 large onion, peeled and quartered
- 2 cloves garlic, peeled and quartered
- 1 tablespoon (15g) olive oil
- 1 carrot, quartered
- 1 teaspoon dried oregano
- 400g lamb mince
- 1 large eggplant, roughly diced
- 400g jar pasta sauce
- 400g can butter beans, drained
- 100g feta cheese

Into the thermo bowl, place onion and garlic.

 5 seconds

 5

Add oil.

 7 minutes

 100°C

 1

Insert butterfly. Add carrot, oregano, mince, eggplant and pasta sauce. Season with sea salt and cracked pepper.

 30 minutes

 100°C

 1

Halfway through, remove the measuring cup and drop in butter beans. Serve scattered with crumbled feta, over orecchiette 'little ears" or rice.

Lamb with Date & Pistachio Salsa

Serves 4

- 4 lamb chops
- 2 oranges, peeled and quartered
- 2 tablespoons (20g) pistachios
- 8 fresh pitted dates
- ½ cup mint

In a nonstick frying pan or on a BBQ, grill the lamb for 4 minutes each side or until done to your liking. Meanwhile place the oranges, pistachios, dates and mint into the thermo bowl.

   3 times

Serve the *Thermo-Licious* salsa on top of each chop with a fresh salad or selection of seasonal veggies.

Salmon Rissoles

Makes 12

- 1 turnip, peeled and chopped
- 2 zucchinis, quartered
- 2 eggs
- 420g can pink salmon, drained
- 1 tablespoon lemon zest
- 1 tablespoon (15g) olive oil

Place the turnip into the thermo bowl.

 5 seconds

 8

Add zucchini, eggs, salmon and zest. Season to taste.

 20 seconds

 4

Using floured hands, roll the mixture into 12 evenly sized cakes. Refrigerate for 20 minutes. Place on a paper-lined baking tray and brush lightly with olive oil. Bake in a preheated 180°C oven for 25 minutes or until golden, turn half way through. *... Thermo-Mazing!*

You Tube 4 Ingredients Channel / Salmon Rissoles

Steamed Chicken & Cashew

Serves 4

- 400g chicken, cut into tenderloins
- 3 tablespoons Gourmet Garden Thai Blend
- 1 litre water
- 1 cup (185g) basmati rice
- 1 carrot, sliced into 1cm discs
- 200g broccoli florets
- ½ cup (60g) raw cashews
- 2 tablespoons ketjap manis

Cover the chicken with the Thai blend and marinate in the fridge for 30 minutes. Place the water in the thermo bowl. Insert the filter basket with rice. Place the veggies in the steamer, first the carrot then the broccoli, then the cashews. Insert the black mesh tray and lay the chicken in it. Cover with the lid.

 18 minutes

Unlock the steamer and set aside. Remove the bowl of rice with the aid of the spatula handle. Spoon even amounts of rice onto plates, drizzle with ketjap manis, top with veggies and chicken and enjoy.

TIP: Ketjap manis is a sweet syrupy soy sauce found in the Asian isle of most major supermarkets ... It's just lovely!

Steamed Fish with Lemongrass & Ginger

Serves 2

- ½ cup (90g) rice
- 1½ cups (375g) water
- 50g beans, top 'n' tailed
- 1 cob of corn, quartered
- 2 white fish fillets
- ¼ teaspoon sea salt
- 2 teaspoons sesame oil
- 5cm piece fresh ginger, peeled, cut into fine strips
- 1 lemongrass stem, pale section only, thinly sliced diagonally
- 4 green shallots, trimmed, thinly sliced diagonally

Put rice into the filter basket. Rinse under running water, then insert into thermo bowl. Cover with water. Into the steamer place the corn and beans. Lock into place on the thermo bowl. Line the steaming mesh with a little wax paper. Sprinkle half the ginger and lemongrass over the paper. Gently score both fish fillets then rub both sides with salt and sesame oil. Place the fish on top of the paper and sprinkle with remaining ginger, lemongrass and shallots. Set into place atop the steaming mesh and pop the lid on.

 16 minutes

Let sit for 5 minutes, then remove the steaming mesh, steamer and filter basket from thermo bowl. Onto a plate, spoon the rice, top with beans and corn, then fish.

*OPTIONAL: Serve drizzled with a deliciously **Soy Garlic Sauce**, whisk together ¼ cup (60g) soy sauce + 1 tablespoon peanut oil + 1 ½ teaspoons fish sauce + 2 garlic cloves, finely chopped, you may need to increase cooking time 12 to 15 minutes or until tender. When adding capsicum add thin broccoli florets and some peas as well ... whatever vegetables you have.*

Thai Chicken Curry

Serves 4

- 270g can coconut milk
- 2 tablespoons (30g) green curry paste
- 100g sliced bamboo shoots
- 90g green beans, cut in half
- 3 tablespoons (45g) fish sauce
- 400g chicken breasts, cut into chunks
- 1 lime, juice and zest
- ½ red capsicum, sliced
- ½ cup freshly torn basil

Place coconut milk into the thermo bowl.

 5 minutes

 100°C

 1

Add the paste, bamboo shoots, beans, fish sauce, chicken, lime juice and zest.

 10 minutes

 100°C

 1

In the last 5 minutes of cooking, remove MC and add capsicum and basil.

SERVING SUGGESTION: Jasmine rice garnished with fresh coriander and sliced chillies.

TIP: To turn this into a vegetarian curry, simply replace chicken with sweet potato, peeled and cubed, you may need to increase cooking time 12 to 15 minutes or until tender. When adding capsicum add thin broccoli florets and some peas as well … whatever vegetables you have.

Tuna Mornay (Dairy-Free)

Serves 4

- 1 clove garlic
- 1 onion, quartered
- 1½ tablespoons (25g) olive oil
- 3½ tablespoons (50g) plain flour
- 1 teaspoon Dijon mustard
- 2 cups (500g) rice milk
- 415g tin of tuna in brine, drained
- ½ cup (70g) frozen peas, thawed
- 125g can creamed corn

Place the garlic and onion into the thermo bowl.

 5 seconds

 7

Scrape down the sides and add oil.

 3 minutes

 90°C

 1

Insert butterfly bar, add remaining 6 ingredients and season well.

 10 minutes

 100°C

 1

SERVING SUGGESTIONS: Take 12 slices of bread and remove crusts, butter lightly and press buttered side into muffin cases. Bake in a 160°C oven for 10 minutes or until just golden, remove and fill with yummy tuna mornay or serve it with pasta or rice.

Veggie-Loaded Bolognaise Sauce

Serves 6

- 2 carrots, chopped
- 1 zucchini, chopped
- 1 onion, peeled and quartered
- 5 mushrooms
- 2 cloves garlic, peeled and chopped
- 2 tablespoons (30g) olive oil
- 400g mince (beef, or a mixture of beef and pork)
- 425g can plum tomatoes
- 1 cup (250g) beef stock
- 2 tablespoons Gourmet Garden Italian Herbs

Place carrots, zucchini, onion, mushrooms and garlic into the thermo bowl.

 10 seconds

 7

Scrape down the sides. Add the oil.

 4 minutes

 90°C

 1

Add the mince.

 5 minutes

 100°C

 1

Add remaining ingredients.

 15 minutes

 100°C

 1

If the sauce starts to spit, simply place the MC on an incline in the lid. Serve with pasta and sprinkled with Parmesan cheese.

TIP: To make your own mince, place 400g meat, cubed and slightly frozen, into the thermo bowl. 10 seconds / Speed 7 or for a chunkier consistency, pulse using the turbo boost function 3-5 times.

RISOTTOS

4-P's RISOTTO
~ Peas, Pesto, Parmesan & Prosciutto

Serves 4

- 1 onion, peeled and chopped
- 2 tablespoons (30g) butter
- 1 cup (185g) Arborio rice, rinsed
- 2½ cups (625g) chicken stock
- ½ cup (125g) white wine
- 1 cup (130g) frozen peas
- 100g Prosciutto, grilled and broken
- ¼ cup (25g) Parmesan (reserve a little for sprinkling)
- ¼ cup (65g) basil pesto
- ¼ cup (40g) pine nuts, toasted

Into the thermo bowl, place onion.

 4 seconds

 7

Add butter and season with cracked pepper.

 3 minutes

 100°C

 1

Insert butterfly. Add rice and ¼ cup (60g) of the stock.

 3 minutes

 100°C

 1

Add remaining stock, wine and peas.

 18 minutes

 100°C

 1

Add prosciutto, Parmesan, pesto, and pine nuts.

 3 minutes

 100°C

 1

Let stand for approx. 10 minutes allowing time for flavours to develop.

OPTIONAL: Serve sprinkled with Parmesan, pine nuts and cracked pepper.

Chicken, Mushroom & Cashew

Serves 4

- 75g Parmesan cheese, cubed
- 1 onion, peeled and quartered
- 2 tablespoons (30g) butter
- 300g chicken breast, cut into 2cm cubes
- 1 cup (185g) Arborio rice
- 3 cups (750g) chicken stock
- 100g mushrooms, sliced
- ½ cup (60g) cashews
- ¼ cup basil leaves, chopped

Place the Parmesan into the thermo bowl.

 4 seconds

 8

Remove and set aside. Add the onion.

 4 seconds

 8

Add the butter and the chicken.

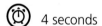 4 minutes

 100°C

 1

Add the stock and rice.

 20 minutes

 90°C

 1

With 6 minutes remaining, remove MC and add the mushrooms and cashews. Replace MC. With 1 minute remaining, add the basil leaves and half the Parmesan cheese. Season to taste and serve immediately sprinkled with remaining Parmesan.

I LOVE LOVE LOVE RISOTTOS

Vary a few ingredients for a different dinner. Some of my favourites;

- *Asparagus and Lemon*
- *Chicken, lemon and rosemary*
- *Mushroom, thyme and Parmesan*
- *Pea, bacon and mint*

Honey Baked Pumpkin

Serves 4

- 500g pumpkin, peeled, cut into 3cm wedges
- 4 tablespoons (60g) olive oil
- 2 tablespoons (30g) honey
- 1 onion, peeled and chopped
- 2 celery stalks, chopped
- 2cm piece fresh ginger, peeled
- 3 cups (750g) vegetable stock
- 1 cup (185g) Arborio rice
- ½ cup chopped flat-leaf parsley, plus extra to garnish

Preheat the oven to 200°C. Lay the pumpkin in an even layer on a large baking tray and drizzle with 2 tablespoons of oil. Season with salt and pepper. Roast for 10 minutes, then remove and drizzle with honey, tossing to coat each piece. Roast for a further 10 minutes until cooked and golden. Set aside.

Place onion, celery and ginger into the thermo bowl.

 5 seconds

 7

Scrape down the sides of thermo, and add the remaining 2 tablespoons of oil.

 4 minutes

 100°C

 1

Lock in butterfly bar. Add the stock and rice.

20 minutes

 90°C

 1

With only 2 minutes remaining, remove MC and add the pumpkin and most of the parsley (use the rest to garnish) and honey, replace MC. Serve immediately.

You Tube 4 Ingredients Channel / Honey Baked Pumpkin Risotto

Spring Risotto

Risottos can be as simple as rice, white wine, stock, and a little Parmesan stirred in at the end, or more elaborate, studded with vegetables, seafood, or meat. To be honest, you can make an endless variety of creamy delicious risottos in your Thermo. Literally, if you have rice and stock, you have a meal!

Serves 4

- 1 medium fennel bulb, trimmed and chopped
- 2 cloves garlic, peeled
- 2 tablespoons (30g) butter
- 8 beans, top 'n' tailed
- 6 asparagus stalks, cut into thirds
- 2 cups English spinach
- ½ cup chopped radishes
- 1 cup (185g) Arborio rice, rinsed
- 3 cups (750g) vegetable stock
- ¼ cup fresh Italian flat leaf parsley
- ¼ cup fresh basil

Into the thermo bowl, place fennel and garlic.

 4 seconds

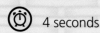 7

Add butter and season with cracked pepper.

(timer) 3 minutes

(temperature) 100°C

(blade) 1

Add beans, asparagus, spinach and radish.

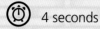 4 seconds

 7

Add rice and stock.

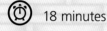 18 minutes

 100°C

 1

With only 4 minutes remaining, remove the MC and add parsley and basil. Let sit for 4 minutes before spooning into bowls. Garnish with fresh herbs to serve.

Sun-dried Tomato with Parmesan & Parma Ham

Serves 4

- 75g Parmesan cheese, cubed
- 1 onion, peeled and quartered
- 2 tablespoons (30g) olive oil
- 3 cups (750g) vegetable stock
- 1 cup (185g) Arborio rice, rinsed
- 8 sun-dried tomatoes
- ¾ cup (100g) frozen peas
- 50g Parma ham, chopped

Place the Parmesan into the thermo bowl.

 4 seconds

 8

Remove and set aside. Add the onion.

 5 seconds

 7

Add the oil.

 3 minutes

 100°C

 1

Lock in butterfly bar. Add the stock and rice.

 20 minutes

 90°C

 1

With only 5 minutes remaining, remove MC and add the sun-dried tomatoes, peas, ham and half the Parmesan. Season to taste and serve immediately sprinkled with remaining Parmesan.

Sweet Strawberry Risotto

Serves 4

- 2 tablespoons unsalted butter
- 1 cup (185g) Arborio rice, rinsed
- 2½ (625g) cups milk
- ⅓ cup (70g) sugar
- 2 teaspoons vanilla extract
- Zest and juice of 1 orange
- 270g can coconut milk
- 300g strawberries, washed, hulled and sliced
- 50g pistachios, chopped

Add butter to the thermo bowl and melt.

 1 minutes

 50°C

 1

Insert butterfly. Add rice and ¼ cup (60g) of milk.

 3 minutes

 100°C

 1

Add all remaining ingredients, except strawberries and pistachios.

 18 minutes

 100°C

 1

Let stand for 10 minutes. Spoon the sliced strawberries into the bottom of small bowls or glasses, top with risotto, garnish with sliced strawberries and a smattering of pistachios.

VEGETARIAN

Cheesy Frittata

*This is also fabulous as a snack or a lunch
with a crisp green salad.*

Serves 6

- 45g Parmesan cheese, cubed
- 1 slice multigrain bread
- 2 cloves garlic
- 1 zucchini, sliced
- 3 eggs
- ½ cup (115g) cream
- Pinch of ground nutmeg
- 2 tablespoons pepitas

Preheat oven 180°C. Line a 20cm quiche dish with baking paper.
Into the thermo bowl, place the Parmesan and bread and garlic.

 4 seconds

 8

Add all remaining ingredients (except pepitas) and season with sea salt
and pepper.

 30 seconds

 4

Pour the mixture into the quiche dish. Sprinkle with pepitas. Bake for
25 minutes. Cool before slicing into wedges to serve.

*OPTIONAL: Dollop with the incredibly flavoursome **Quick-Fire Tomato Jam** p. 111.*

Gnocchi

Serves 6

- 1½ cups (260g) plain flour
- 250g ricotta
- 1 large egg yolk

Place all the ingredients into the thermo bowl.

 2 minutes

 3

Using a teaspoon roll the mixture into balls. Traditional gnocchi has ridges, so that the sauce sticks! So to create the ridges, press each piece of dough against the tines of a fork. Bring a large saucepan of water to the boil. Add the gnocchi and cook for about 2 to 3 minutes or until they float. Remove with a large slotted spoon and drain well. Serve immediately, tossed together with your favourite sauce.

 4 Ingredients Channel / Gnocchi

FORMAGGIO SAUCE

- 1 cup (250g) sour cream
- ¼ cup (60g) butter
- 25g gorgonzola
- 50g Parmesan cheese, cubed
- 100g mascarpone
- 50g mozzarella cheese

Pop all the ingredients into the thermo bowl.

 4 minutes

 100°C

 4

Homemade Tomato Sugo

Makes 1 litre

- 1 carrot
- 1 Spanish onion
- 2 sticks celery
- 3 cloves garlic
- 3 tablespoons (45g) olive oil
- 1kg Roma tomatoes, chopped, discarding seeds
- 375g jar tomato paste
- 1 tablespoon (12g) brown sugar
- 2 cups (500g) vegetable stock

Add the carrot, onion, celery and garlic to thermo bowl.

 10 seconds

 8

Add olive oil and season with sea salt and pepper.

 4 minutes

 100°C

 1

Add the tomatoes, tomato paste, brown sugar and stock.

 20 minutes

 70°C

 2

SERVING SUGGESTION: Serve this with your family's favourite pasta (ravioli is ours), over meatballs, on meatloaf, with lasagne or polenta.

Macaroni & Cheese with a 'Veggie-Twist'

Serves 6

- 300g macaroni, *cooked*
- 90g cheddar cheese, cubed
- 50g Parmesan, cubed
- 200g cauliflower, roughly chopped
- 1 carrot, roughly chopped
- 1 zucchini, roughly chopped
- ½ an onion, peeled and chopped
- 1 cup (250g) vegetable stock
- 75g butter
- 4 tablespoons (60g) plain flour
- 1½ cups (375g) milk

Place the cheeses into the thermo bowl (otherwise use 1 cup grated cheddar and ½ cup grated Parmesan).

 10 seconds

 8

Pour into a bowl and set aside. Place the vegetables and veggie stock into the thermo bowl.

 5 minutes

 100°C

 3

Turbo boost for 3 seconds for a puree. Set aside. Rinse bowl. Place butter and flour into the thermo bowl. Use the spatula to brush the flour from the blades.

 6 minutes

90°C

1

Preheat oven 180°C. Add the milk, giving the sauce a little stir with the spatula.

 7 minutes

90°C

4

Add ¾ of the cheeses and season with sea salt and cracked pepper.

 2 minutes

90°C

4

Combine pasta, veggie puree and cheese sauce in a large bowl. Pour into a pie dish, sprinkle with remaining cheese and bake for 20 minutes or until golden, bubbling, crispy and delicious.

Mediterranean Pasta Sauce

Serves 8

- 2 onions, peeled and quartered
- 2 tablespoons (30g) butter
- 4 tomatoes
- 50g pitted black olives
- 1 cured chorizo, sliced

Place the onions into the thermo bowl, spreading evenly around the blade.

 5 seconds

 7

Add the butter.

 4 minutes

 90°C

 1

Add tomatoes.

 4 seconds

 4

Add the olives and chorizo.

 8 minutes

 90°C

 2

Serve with your favourite pasta, sprinkled with Parmesan cheese.

Pumpkin & Lentil Curry

Makes 4

- 2 tablespoons (40g) red curry paste
- 400g can coconut milk
- 250g pumpkin, peeled and sliced
- 400g can brown lentils, washed and drained
- 12 snow peas, sliced
- ½ cup fresh coriander

Place curry paste and a quarter of the coconut milk into the thermo bowl.

 2 minutes

 60°C

 1

Add remaining coconut milk, pumpkin and lentils.

 15 minutes

 100°C

 1

With 6 minutes remaining, remove MC and add snow peas. Replace MC. In the last minute of cooking, remove MC and add the coriander.

SERVING SUGGESTION: Steamed jasmine rice with fresh coriander and sliced red chillies or spring onions for colour and crunch.

Ratatouille Stew

Serves 4

- 1 onion, quartered
- 4 garlic cloves, peeled
- 1 capsicum, quartered and deseeded
- 2 tablespoons (30g) olive oil
- 300g eggplant, diced
- 2 zucchinis, diced
- 3 tomatoes, chopped
- 1 tablespoon (20g) tomato paste
- 1 tablespoon fresh thyme
- ¼ cup chopped fresh basil

Into the thermo bowl, place the onions, garlic, and capsicum.

 5 seconds

 5

Scrape down the sides of the bowl with the spatula. Add olive oil.

 4 minutes

 90°C

 1

Add eggplant, zucchinis, tomatoes and tomato paste. Season to taste.

 20 minutes

 90°C

 1

With 5 minutes remaining remove MC and add the thyme and basil. Serve with rice and sprinkled with Parmesan or use any leftovers the next day as a divine pizza sauce, sprinkle with feta and drizzle with balsamic vinegar to create your very own Ratatouille Pizza!

Spinach & Feta Quiche

Serves 6

- 1 sheet puff pastry
- 50g Parmesan cheese, cubed
- 1 clove garlic
- 150g English spinach
- 1 cup (250g) sour cream
- 4 eggs
- 2 sprigs of dill
- 100g feta, crumbled

Heat oven to 180°C. Line a 20cm quiche dish with baking paper and then puff pastry. Gently press the pastry to fit into the flat of the base. Bake in oven for 15 minutes. Place the Parmesan into the thermo bowl.

 4 seconds

 8

Remove half and set to one side. Add the garlic.

 3 seconds

 7

Add spinach, sour cream, eggs and dill. Season to taste

 5 seconds

 7

This results in a runny texture. Sprinkle feta into the pre-baked pastry case, then pour over the mixture. Sprinkle with reserved Parmesan and bake for 25 minutes or until golden. Note, this quiche will not hold its rise as it has no flour, it will rise and fall.

*TIP: See **Sausage Rolls** p. 120 on how to make your own puff pastry.*

Steamed Veggie Dim Sims

Serves 4

- 1 litre water
- 1 cup (185g) basmati rice
- 1 cob of corn, cut into quarters
- 1 carrot, sliced
- 50g broccolini
- 660g Vegetable Dim Sims

Place the water into the thermo bowl and insert the rice basket. Place the corn, then the carrot and broccolini in the steamer basket. Then the Dim Sims into the black mesh tray, and add the lid.

  15 minutes

Then drizzle with this lovely sauce.

ASIAN DIPPING SAUCE

- ½ cup (125g) vegetable oil
- ¼ cup (50g) sugar
- 1 tablespoon (15g) tamari soya sauce
- 2 tablespoons (30g) red wine vinegar

Combine all ingredients and whisk.

Veggie Rissoles

Makes 8

- 1 cup (160g) cashews
- 2 slices wholegrain bread, torn
- 1 carrot, chopped
- 1 small brown onion, peeled and quartered
- 1 garlic clove, peeled
- 1 zucchini, chopped
- 4 stalks parsley, stalks removed
- 125g tofu, sliced
- 1 tablespoon (15g) soy sauce
- 1 tablespoon (15g) honey
- ½ cup (85g) plain flour
- ½ cup (125g) olive oil

Place the cashews and bread into the thermo bowl.

 5 seconds

 7

Remove and set aside. Add the carrot, onion and garlic into the thermo bowl.

 5 seconds

 9

Add zucchini, parsley, tofu, soy sauce and honey along with cashews and bread.

 30 seconds

 3

Sprinkle the flour onto a plate and season with sea salt and pepper. Using damp hands, roll the mixture into 8 even-sized balls and coat in flour. Over medium heat, place the oil in a nonstick frying pan and cook for 3 to 4 minutes on each side or until golden and cooked through.

SIDES

Cauliflower Mash

Serves 4

- 30g Parmesan cheese, cubed
- ½ head cauliflower, broken into florets
- 1 garlic clove, peeled
- ¾ cup (185g) vegetable stock

Place the Parmesan into the thermo bowl.

 5 seconds

 8

Remove and set aside. Place the cauliflower and garlic into the thermo bowl.

 4 times

Scrape down the sides of thermo bowl with the spatula. Add the stock, Parmesan and season with cracked black pepper.

 12 minutes

 100°C

 1

Adjust seasoning to taste.

OPTIONAL: Into the stainless steel steamer, place a sliced carrot and 12 broccoli florets. Secure with the lid, then cook 12 minutes / Cook Mode … this way you get some nutritious steamed veggies at the same time!

Creamy Polenta

Serves 4

- 80g Parmesan cheese, cubed
- 8 sage leaves
- 2 cups (500g) milk
- 2 cups (500g)water
- 1 tablespoon (15g) olive oil
- 200g polenta
- 3 tablespoons (45g) butter

Place the Parmesan and sage into the thermo bowl.

 5 seconds

 8

Remove and set aside. Add the milk, water, oil and polenta and season to taste. With just 1 minute remaining, remove MC and add the cheese and butter replace MC.

 9 minutes

 100°C

 4

Serve immediately.

*SERVING SUGGESTIONS: This is totally lovely served with grilled lamb chops, or grilled chicken with sautéed mushrooms and thyme, or **Ratatouille Stew** p. 186.*

Mashed Potato

Serves 6

- 1kg potatoes, peeled and chopped into 2cm cubes
- 1 cup (250g) milk
- ¼ teaspoon sea salt
- 30g butter

Place the milk, salt and potatoes into the thermo bowl.

 20 minutes

 100°C

 1

Add the butter, and season to taste.

 1 minute

 3

Remove the lid and cool for 5 minutes before serving.

Mashed potatoes are very versatile. Vary with these suggestions:
- *Sour cream and grated Parmesan cheese*
- *Dijon mustard and finely chopped rosemary*
- *1 tablespoon of pesto, great with grilled chicken*
- *2 tablespoons freshly chopped mint or mint sauce to serve with roast and grilled lamb ...* Thermo-Licious

Stamppot

Serves 4

- 2 carrots, peeled and sliced into 2cm pieces
- ½ Swede, peeled and diced
- ½ parsnip, peeled and diced
- 2 cups (500g) vegetable stock
- ¼ teaspoon ground nutmeg

Place vegetables and stock into the thermo bowl.

 20 minutes

 100°C

 1

Add nutmeg.

 10 seconds

 8

Season to taste with freshly ground pepper.

SERVING SUGGESTIONS: This is just delicious served as a side with grilled meat and steamed greens or as a main. Pour the mixture into a pie dish and sprinkle with grated cheddar cheese. Bake in a 180°C oven for 15 minutes or until golden and serve with buttery corn on the cob and steamed greens.

Desserts

Enjoying a delicious dessert is one of life's simple pleasures. With a Thermo you can remove the stress and mess with a selection of sweets ranging from Nana's Impossible Pie to Strawberry Soft Serve, Passionfruit Cheescake to a wonderful Walnut Cake.

CAKES & PUDDINGS

Butterscotch Pudding

Serves 8

- 1½ cup (300g) brown sugar
- 200g butter
- 2 eggs
- 2 cups (350g) self-raising flour
- 2 tablespoons (40g) golden syrup
- 2 tablespoons (35g) cornflour
- 2½ cups (625g) boiling water

Preheat oven to 180°C. Grease a 30 x 20cm rectangular baking dish and set aside. Place half a cup of sugar and butter into the thermo bowl.

 3 minutes

 100°C

 1

Add eggs, self-raising flour and golden syrup.

 25 seconds

 5

Using the spatula, pour the mixture into the baking dish. Then into the thermo bowl, add 1 cup of brown sugar, cornflour and boiling water.

 4 seconds

 3

Pour the sauce over the back of a serving spoon onto the cake and bake for 40 to 45 minutes or until golden and bubbling.

Red Velvet Cupcakes

Makes 16

- ⅓ cup (80g) butter, cubed
- 400g can condensed milk
- 1 cup (170g) self-raising flour
- 1 egg
- 2 tablespoons (16g) cocoa powder
- 1 tablespoon red food colouring

Preheat oven to 180°C. Line 16 cupcake tins with papers. Place all the ingredients into the thermo bowl.

 2 minutes

 4

Spoon the mixture into the cupcake cases and bake for 15 minutes. Stand the cakes in the pans for 2 minutes. Transfer to a wire rack to cool.

OPTIONAL: Top with **Cream Cheese Frosting** *p. 230.*

Sticky Date Pudding

Debbie Wuoti is the owner of TM Essentials,
www.tm-essentials.com.au *is an online store selling*
all kinds of fabulous accessories for your Thermo-Appliance.

Serves 4

- 1¼ cups (210g) dates, seeded
- 1 cup (250g) boiling water
- 1 teaspoon bi-carb soda
- ½ cup (100g) brown sugar
- ¼ cup (60g) butter
- 2 eggs
- ¾ cup (140g) self-raising flour (or plain with 1 teaspoon of baking powder)

Preheat oven to 180°C. Grease a 20cm square tin or a muffin tray. In the thermo bowl, combine dates, boiling water and soda and let stand for 5 minutes. Add sugar and butter.

 10 seconds

 7

Scrape down and add flour first, then eggs.

 5 seconds

 5

Repeat until combined. Pour into prepared tin or large muffin cups (makes 9 large muffins). Bake for 15 to 17 minutes in a moderate oven for muffins and 20 to 25 for larger tin. Stand for 5 minutes before turning out. Serve with *Thermost* amazing sauce on the following page

Caramel Sauce

Makes 1½ cups

- ⅔ cup (140g) brown sugar
- 100g butter
- 250g cream

Place all ingredients into the thermo bowl.

⏲ 6 minutes

🌡 100°C

✳ 3

Sauce will thicken on standing.

Traybake Chocolate Cake

Serves 12

- 1 cup (112g) cocoa powder
- ¾ cup (185g) boiling water
- ¾ teaspoon bicarbonate soda
- 1¼ cups (250g) raw sugar
- 4 eggs
- ¾ cup (180g) vegetable oil
- 1 generous cup (200g) self-raising flour

Mix the cocoa with boiling water, whisk in the bicarbonate of soda and set aside for 20 minutes to cool. Preheat oven 180°C. Line a 30 x 20cm baking tray with baking paper. Pour the sugar into the thermo bowl.

 10 seconds

 8

Add the eggs and oil.

 20 seconds

 5

Add the flour and cocoa mixture.

 20 seconds

 6

Pour the mixture into the prepared tray and bake for 35 minutes or until risen and firm, and an inserted skewer comes out clean. Cool before icing.

*OPTIONAL: This is visually spectacular (and a whole lot naughty) topped with **Dreamy Chocolate Icing** p. 232 and a smattering of Smarties.*

Tiramisu

Serves 6

- ¼ cup (50g) sugar
- 300g whipping cream
- 200g mascarpone cheese
- 200g sponge cake (store-bought)
- ½ cup (125g) freshly brewed coffee
- 2 tablespoons (30g) Kahlua
- 1 tablespoon (8g) cocoa powder

Into the thermo bowl, place the sugar.

 10 seconds

 8

Insert the butterfly bar over the sharp, lower blade and add the cream.

 20 seconds

 4

Remove the butterfly bar, scrape down the sides and add the mascarpone.

 20 seconds

 5

Slice the sponge into 1cm thick slices. Mix together coffee and Kahlua. Into a 20cm dish lay 4 slices of sponge and drizzle with 2 tablespoons of the coffee mix. Spread a layer of sweet cream over the sponge. Repeat the layers three times, ending with cream. Sift over with cocoa powder to densely cover the final layer of cream. Leave this covered in the fridge for 2 hours before serving.

Walnut & Lemon Cake

Serves 8

- 350g walnuts
- 1 cup (200g) raw sugar
- 4 eggs, room temperature
- 1 lemon, zest

Preheat oven 180°C. Line a 20cm springform cake tin with baking paper. Place the walnuts into the thermo bowl.

 10 seconds

 9

Remove and set aside. Wipe the bowl clean. Pour the sugar into the thermo bowl.

 10 seconds

 9

Insert the butterfly bar over the sharp, lower blade. Add the eggs.

 6 minutes

 37°C

 1

Repeat the process without the Temperature, so you are beating for a total of 12 minutes. Remove the butterfly bar. Add the walnuts and the entire zest of one lemon.

 30 seconds

 1

Pour into the prepared cake tin and bake for 55 to 60 minutes. Allow to cool before removing from the tin.

OPTIONAL: Serve topped with **Butterscotch** *or* **Espresso Cream** *p. 228.*

Whole Orange Cake

Serves 8

- 1 orange, skin on and quartered (remove seeds)
- 1 cup (230g) butter
- 3 eggs
- 1 cup (200g) sugar
- 2 cups (350g) self-raising flour

Preheat oven 180°C. Line a 20cm springform cake tin with baking paper. Place the orange and butter into the thermo bowl.

 10 seconds

 8

Add the remaining ingredients.

 20 seconds

 4

Pour the mixture into the cake tin. Bake for 50 minutes or until cooked.

TIP: An easy way to check if your cake is cooked is to insert a toothpick in the middle of the cake and have it come out clean.

CHEESECAKES & TARTS

Cheesecake Bases

Base 1

- 1 cup (160g) raw almonds
- 10 pitted dates
- ½ cup (60g) moist coconut flakes

Place all ingredients into the thermo bowl.

 20 seconds

 8

Using the spatula, scrape the mixture out into a 20cm pie dish, press it into the corners of the base and chill for at least 30 minutes.

Base 2

- 1½ cups (250g) plain flour
- 125g chilled butter, cubed
- ⅓ cup (80g) caster sugar
- 1 egg yolk
- 2 tablespoon (30g) chilled water

Combine flour, butter and caster sugar into the thermo bowl.

 10 seconds

 7

When the mixture is looking like breadcrumbs, add the egg yolk and water.

 25 seconds

Using the spatula scrape the dough into a paper-lined pie dish and press into place. Add some nutmeg or cinnamon for flavour.

Chocolate Swirl Cheesecake

Serves 10

- ½ cup (100g) caster sugar
- 250g cream cheese, chopped
- 300g sour cream
- 2 eggs
- 75g dark chocolate, melted

Preheat oven 180°C. Place the sugar into the thermo bowl.

 10 seconds

 8

Add cream cheese, sour cream and eggs.

 2 minutes

 4

Scrape down sides. Pour half the cheesecake filling into a prepared cheesecake base. Drizzle with half the melted chocolate, and using a butter knife 'swirl' it through the creamy mixture. Add remaining cheesecake filling and melted chocolate and 'swirl'. Bake for 1 hour, then turn off the oven and let it cool. Refrigerate and serve cold.

Citron Tarts

OMG ... These are Thermo-Mazing!

Makes 6

- 1 sheet shortcrust pastry
- 1 lemon, peeled, quartered and seeds removed
- ½ cup (100g) caster sugar
- 3 eggs
- 2 tablespoons (30g) butter

From the pastry cut 6 rounds and mould each into a cupcake tin. Bake in a 180°C oven for 5 to 6 minutes or until just golden. Place the lemon segments into the thermo bowl.

 5 seconds

Scrape down the sides. Add sugar and eggs.

 7 minutes

 70°C

 2

With 1 minute remaining remove the MC and add the butter to the mixture. Cool slightly, then pour the lemon curd into the pastry cases. They will set in the cooling process.

Honey Crunch Cheescakes

Makes 12

- 2 shortcrust pastry sheets
- 6 Butternut Snap biscuits
- 250g light cream cheese, softened
- ⅓ cup (100g) honey
- 100g thickened cream

Preheat oven 180°C. Cut one sheet of pastry into thirds vertically, then horizontally, creating 9 squares. From the second sheet, cut a one-third strip vertically, and from it three squares. Return the remainder of that sheet to the freezer. Into a nonstick muffin tray, gently line each of the 12 holes with a square of pastry. Bake for 10 minutes or until golden, allow to cool.

Meanwhile, place the biscuits into the thermo bowl.

 4 seconds

 4

Remove from bowl and set aside. Clean the bowl. Add cream cheese, honey and cream.

 10 seconds

 8

Using the spatula, scrape mixture down onto blades

 10 seconds

 5

Spoon the creamy mixture evenly between the pastry cases. Sprinkle with the Butternut Snap biscuit crumbs and serve immediately.

Honey Ricotta Cheesecake with Blueberry Coulis

Serves 10

Filling

- 1½ cups (375g) Greek yoghurt
- 250g ricotta cheese
- ¼ cup (80g) honey
- 1 teaspoon vanilla extract
- 2 eggs
- 1 teaspoon grated lemon zest

Coulis

- 1 cup (140g) frozen blueberries
- ¼ cup (60g) water
- 1 teaspoon vanilla extract

Preheat oven 150°C. Place the yoghurt, ricotta and honey into the thermo bowl.

 30 seconds

 3

Add 1 teaspoon of vanilla, the egg and lemon zest.

 2 minutes

 4

Pour the filling into a prepared cheesecake base and bake for 45 to 50 minutes or until the filling is set. Cool the cheesecake and then refrigerate for at least 4 hours. To serve, top with a simple Blueberry Coulis. Place the blueberries, water and vanilla into a small saucepan. Bring to the boil then reduce the heat and simmer for 2 minutes. Remove from the heat and cool. Pour the mixture into the thermo bowl and turbo boost for 3 seconds. Pour over the cheesecake to serve.

Passionfruit Cheesecake

Serves 10

- 250g cream cheese, softened
- 400g can condensed milk
- 10g gelatin
- 2 passionfruit

Add cream cheese to the thermo bowl.

 10 seconds

 8

Scrape down the sides. Add condensed milk.

 2 minutes

 4

Add the gelatin to ¼ cup of hot water and stir briskly with a fork until dissolved. Add it and passionfruit pulp to the creamy mixture.

 30 seconds

 2

Pour this mixture over the base and return to the refrigerator. Chill for at least 4 hours before serving.

Creamy Citrus Rice Pudding

Serves 4

- 1 litre milk
- 1 cup (185g) Arborio rice
- ¼ cup (50g) raw sugar
- 1 teaspoon vanilla extract
- 2 tablespoons orange zest

Insert the butterfly bar over the sharp, lower blade. Place all the ingredients into the thermo bowl.

 20 minutes

 100°C

 1

Check for texture, taste and tenderness, and serve sprinkled with a little extra orange zest. Please note, this will thicken as it cools.

TIP: To make your own Shortcrust Pastry: Place ½ cup (115g) butter, chilled and cubed, 1 generous cup (220g) plain flour, and a pinch of salt into the thermo bowl. Mix 10 seconds / Speed 7. Add ¼ cup (60g) icy cold water and knead for 20 seconds. Add a little extra water to bind if needed. Refrigerate for 15 minutes before rolling out.

Nana's Impossible Pie

Serves 8

- 4 eggs
- ½ cup (85g) plain flour
- 2 cups (500g) milk
- 1 cup (200g) sugar
- 1 cup (120g) desiccated coconut
- 2 teaspoons vanilla extract

Preheat oven 180°C. Place all the ingredients into the thermo bowl.

 2 minutes

 4

Pour the mixture into a 20cm paper-lined pie dish. Bake for 1 hour or until golden and set in the centre. The milk and eggs form a custard, and the other ingredients form the base and topping while baking.

Pecan Pie

Serves 6

- 1 cup (200g) sugar
- 1 cup (130g) pecans
- 20 Jatz crackers
- 3 egg whites

Preheat oven 180°C. Into the thermo bowl, place the sugar.

 10 seconds

 8

Remove and set aside. Into the uncleaned bowl, add the pecans and Jatz.

 4 seconds

Remove, and set aside. Clean the bowl and dry very well. Insert the butterfly, then add the egg whites.

 10 minutes

 2

After 2 minutes, remove MC and gradually start to add the sugar, so that all of it is added by 8 minutes, leaving a couple of minutes to fully incorporate. Remove the butterfly. Add back the pecans and Jatz.

 20 seconds

 1

Using the spatula, scrape the mixture into a 22cm paper-lined cake tin.
Bake for 25 minutes, in the bottom third of the oven, until nice and golden.

SERVING SUGGESTION: Top with freshly whipped cream and sliced strawberries.

Toblerone Cheesecake

*Yep, you read it right! My gorgeous neighbour
Janice introduced me to this recipe and we've been
at the gym together ever since ~ haha!*

Serves 10

- 250g Chocolate Ripple biscuits
- 5 tablespoons (75g) butter, melted
- 200g Toblerone
- 375g cream cheese
- 160g tub of dolloping cream
- ¼ cup (50g) sugar

Line a 22cm cake tin with baking paper, or grease with butter, set aside. Into the thermo bowl, place the biscuits.

 1 second (repetitions)

until a fine meal results. Pour the crumbs into a bowl and add the melted butter, mix well to combine. Press into prepared cake tin and pop into freezer for 5 minutes. Wipe clean thermo bowl and add Toblerone pieces.

 2 minutes

 37°C

 3

Add remaining ingredients.

 1 minute

 4

Using the spatula, give a couple of stirs before scraping the mixture onto the biscuit crumb base. Return to the freezer for 45 minutes. Slice to serve studded with freshly sliced strawberries. Keep refrigerated for 2 to 3 days.

CHOCOLATE, ICE-CREAMS & OTHER LOVELIES

Baileys Zabaglione

Makes 4

- ½ cup (100g) caster sugar
- 2 eggs
- 4 egg yolks
- ¾ cup (185g) Baileys Irish liqueur

Insert the butterfly over the sharp, lower blade and add the sugar, eggs and egg yolks.

🕙 4 minutes

⊕ 4

Add the Baileys.

🕙 5 minutes

🌡 70°C

⊕ 4

Serve immediately in 4 x half-cup glasses or ramekins.

TIP: With remaining egg whites make a Pavlova, meringues, macaroons, or a healthy egg white omelette. Remember they also freeze beautifully, just as good thawed as they are fresh!

Banana & PB Soft Serve

Serves 4

- 3 large, frozen ripe bananas, chopped
- 3 tablespoons (45g) peanut butter
- ¼ teaspoon vanilla extract
- ¼ teaspoon cinnamon
- Pinch of sea salt

Place the ingredients into the thermo bowl.

 30 seconds

 8

Serve immediately.

OPTIONAL: Serve with a sprinkle of crushed roasted peanuts, or place back in the freezer. If you do refreeze, run it through the thermo again (30 seconds, speed 8) before serving will help keep its yummy creaminess.

Blueberry Cheesecake Ice-cream

Serves 4

- ½ packet (125g) Scotch Finger biscuits
- 3 cups (450g) frozen blueberries
- 4 tablespoons condensed milk
- 125g cream cheese

Place Scotch Fingers into the thermo bowl.

  3 seconds

Set aside to add in later. Place the blueberries and condensed milk into the thermo bowl.

 3 seconds

Add the cream cheese and biscuit crumbs.

  3 seconds

Serve immediately.

OPTIONAL: I have also made this to the delight of many using Butternut Snap biscuits.

Chocolate Caramel Slice
Slice Baby!

"This is THE Caramel Slice that will leave EVERYONE wanting more!" Said Debbie Wuoti from TM Essentials, **www.tm-essentials.com.au** *an online store selling all kinds of accessories for your Thermo-Appliance.*

Makes 24

For the base

- ½ cup (120g) butter
- 1 cup (170g) plain flour
- ¾ cup (160g) brown sugar
- 1 cup (100g) desiccated coconut
- 1 teaspoon baking powder

For the caramel

- 400g can condensed milk
- 3 tablespoons (45g) golden syrup
- 2 tablespoons (30g) butter

For the topping

- 120g milk chocolate
- 50g dark chocolate

Line a 20 x 30cm slice tray with baking paper. Preheat the oven to 180°C. Into the thermo bowl, place the butter.

 3 minutes

 90°C

 2

Add the remaining base ingredients.

 15 seconds

 3

Press the base into the slice tin and bake for 10 minutes or until golden brown. Wash and dry the thermo bowl. Add condensed milk, syrup and butter.

 10 minutes

 100°C

 2

Pour over the cooked base and return to the oven for a further 10 minutes. Remove and allow to cool. Wash and dry the thermo bowl. Add the milk and dark chocolates.

 3 minutes

 90°C

 2

Spread over the top of the caramel. Allow to cool. Slice into 24 pieces. Keep refrigerated for 4 to 5 days.

Egg Custard

This is *Thermost* delicious custard I've ever made.

Makes approx. 4 cups

- ½ cup (90g) raw sugar
- 3 tablespoons (30g) cornflour
- 3 eggs
- 2 cups (500g) milk
- 1 teaspoon vanilla extract

Place the sugar and cornflour into the thermo bowl.

 5 seconds

 9

Add eggs, milk and vanilla extract.

 7 minutes

 90°C

 3

This results in a delicious creamy pouring custard and is just lovely with puddings, especially the **4** Ingredient Plum Pudding in **4 Ingredients Celebrations at Christmas**. Or over freshly sliced bananas, sprinkled with nutmeg or in a bowl just on its own.

Frozen Banana Ice-cream with Chocolate Sauce

Serves 2

- 3 frozen bananas, chopped
- 1 tablespoon (15g) coconut oil
- 1 tablespoon (8g) cocoa powder
- 1 teaspoon agave nectar
- 2 teaspoons almond butter

Pop the bananas into the thermo bowl.

 30 seconds

 8

Meanwhile, in a small bowl, quickly whisk coconut oil, cocoa powder and agave nectar until nice and smooth. Then spoon the creamy ice-cream into a bowl and drizzle with the sauce and a dollop of almond butter.

OPTIONAL: Substitute almond butter for crushed almonds, strawberries or blueberries.

Healthy Raspberry Mousse

Serves 4

- 225g fresh raspberries
- 350g silken tofu
- ½ teaspoon vanilla extract
- 3 tablespoons (60g) agave nectar or honey

Insert the butterfly, locking it in over the sharp, lower blade. Place the ingredients into the thermo bowl.

 1 minute

 8

Pour the mixture evenly among 4 dessert dishes or glasses and chill for up to 2 hours.

SERVING SUGGESTION: Garnish with a few raspberries and a green mint leaf to serve.

Turkish Delight Panna Cotta

Makes 4

- ¼ cup (50g) sugar
- 300g cream
- ½ cup (125g) milk
- ¼ cup (60g) water
- ½ teaspoon rosewater
- 150g Turkish delight, chopped
- 10g sachet of gelatin

Place the sugar into the thermo bowl.

 10 seconds

 8

Add cream, milk, water, rosewater and Turkish delight.

 8 minutes

 90°C

 2

Mix the gelatin into ¼ cup of hot water to dissolve. Add to the cream mixture.

 1 minute

 100°C

 2

Pour the mix into 4 tall champagne flutes. Refrigerate until set.

TIP: To serve garnish with white chocolate shards, fresh strawberries or edible flowers.

Strawberry Soft Serve

Serves 2

- 300g frozen strawberries, or any frozen fruit
- ½ cup (100g) caster sugar
- ⅔ cup (150g) thickened cream

Place the frozen strawberries into the thermo bowl.

 10 seconds

 10

Scrape down the sides. Insert the butterfly, locking it in over the sharp, lower blade. Add the sugar and cream.

 30 seconds

 4

Serve immediately as a delicious soft serve, or freeze for up to one week.

Tempering Chocolate

Tempering chocolate is a method of heating and cooling chocolate in order to use it for coating, moulding or dipping.
It gives the chocolate a smooth and glossy finish, and is done best at around 37°C. Your Thermo is the ideal appliance for tempering chocolate perfectly!

Makes 2 cups

* **380g chocolate melts**

Place the chocolate into the thermo bowl.

 4 minutes

 37°C

 2

Half way, pause and scrape down the sides of the bowl if required.

Tim Tam Truffles

Makes 24

- 1 packet (200g) Tim Tam biscuits
- 4 tablespoons (80g) cream cheese
- 200g dark chocolate melts

Line a tray with wax paper. Place Tim Tams into the thermo bowl.

 20 seconds

 6

Add the cream cheese.

 1 minute

 3

Or until combined, there should be no traces of white. Using a teaspoon roll into 24 balls, place on tray and refrigerate. Wash and dry the thermo bowl. Add the chocolate melts.

 2 minutes

 37°C

 3

Pour the chocolate into a large bowl. Using forks, dip the Tim Tam balls into the melted chocolate, allow excess chocolate to drip away. Place back onto the tray and when all are coated, refrigerate to set.

AMAZING ICINGS

Butterscotch Cream

Makes 1 cup

- 250g mascarpone
- 1 generous tablespoon (25g) golden syrup
- 2½ tablespoons (20g) icing sugar
- Pinch of ground cinnamon

Insert butterfly. Place all ingredients into the thermo bowl.

 30 seconds

 4

Chill until required. And for a yummy variation, try this next recipe.

Espresso Cream

Makes 1 cup

- 250g mascarpone
- 1 tablespoon (15g) espresso
- 1 generous tablespoon (25g) golden syrup
- 2½ tablespoons (20g) icing sugar

Insert the butterfly bar. Place all ingredients into the thermo bowl.

 30 seconds

 4

Chill until required.

Cashew Icing

Makes 1 cup

- 1 cup (160g) raw cashews, soaked for 2 hours
  (reserve 2 tablespoons of water, discard the rest)
- 1 tablespoon (20g) agave nectar, or honey
- 1 teaspoon fresh lemon juice
- ½ teaspoon vanilla extract
- 1½ tablespoons (25g) coconut oil

Place all the ingredients, including the reserved cashew water, into the thermo bowl.

 5 seconds

Scrape down the sides with the spatula.

 1 minute

 5

*SERVING SUGGESTIONS: This is just AMAZE-A-TOID served on **Whole Orange Cake** p. 203, carrot cake, pineapple cake or muffins, pancakes or just about anything really!!!!*

Cream Cheese Frosting

Makes approx. 2 cups

- 1½ cups (300g) sugar
- 125g cream cheese, softened
- ¼ cup (55g) butter, softened
- 1 tablespoon (15g) milk

Place the sugar into the thermo bowl.

 10 seconds

 8

Add the remaining ingredients.

 40 seconds

 4

Use the spatula if needed to scape down sides and pulse to blend.
Spread onto cooled cakes, cupcakes or muffins.

You Tube *4 Ingredients Channel / Cream Cheese Frosting*

Dreamy Chocolate Icing

Makes 1 cup

- 1½ cups (300g) raw sugar
- ½ cup (115g) butter, softened
- 1 teaspoon vanilla extract
- 2 tablespoons (16g) cocoa powder

Place the raw sugar into the thermo bowl.

 20 seconds

 10

Insert butterfly bar. Add the remaining 3 ingredients.

 1 minute

 4

Using the spatula, scrape down the sides, pushing the mixture over the blades.

 30 seconds

 4

Homemade Icing Sugar

Makes 1 cup

- 1 cup (220g) sugar

Place the sugar into the thermo bowl.

 10 seconds

 8

Store in an airtight container.

TIP: To turn sugar into caster sugar reduce the milling time to 3 seconds … Easy!

All thermos offer a super simple way to turn sugar into caster sugar and then icing sugar in seconds.

You will be Thermo-Mazed!

Rosewater Buttercream

Makes 1 cup

- ½ cup (115g) butter, chopped
- 2 cups (240g) icing sugar
- 2 tablespoons cream
- 1 teaspoon rose essence
- 3 to 4 drops rose colouring
- Pinch of sea salt

Place the butter into the thermo bowl.

 10 seconds

 4

Add remaining ingredients.

 15 seconds

 4

Using the spatula, scrape down the sides of the bowl.

 15 seconds

 4

When nice and smooth, use to frost your favourite sponge or the delectable **10-Second Coconut Bread** on p. 16.

Salted Peanut Frosting

Makes 3 cups

- 100g salted roasted peanuts
- 200g cream cheese, softened
- 4 cups (480g) icing sugar
- 50g butter, softened

Place the peanuts into the thermo bowl.

 4 seconds (or until they resemble breadcrumbs)

 10

Add the cream cheese, icing sugar and butter.

 2 minutes

 2

Scrape down the sides. Store in an air-tight container in the refrigerator until ready to use.

SERVING SUGGESTIONS: This is Thermo-Licious spread over chocolate brownies, sandwiched between cookies or on a freshly baked chocolate cake.

ThermoBambino

Delicious and nutritious baby
recipes made in minutes;
cooked, boiled or steamed your
little ThermoBambino will be
ever so thankful for your efforts.

Apple & Pear with Cinnamon

Makes 2 cups

- 2 medium apples, peeled, cored, and chopped
- 2 medium pears, peeled, cored, and chopped
- 1 cup (250g) water
- Generous pinch of ground cinnamon (optional)

Place all the ingredients into the thermo bowl.

 4 minutes

 100°C

 1

Before serving.

 10 seconds

 8

Banana & Blueberry Quinoa Purée

Makes 1½ cups

- ⅓ cup (70g) quinoa
- ⅔ cup (160ml) water
- ⅔ cup (100g) blueberries
- 1 banana (200g), chopped
- 1 tablespoon water (extra)

Place quinoa in a fine sieve and rinse under cold running water. Drain well. Combine quinoa and the water in a small saucepan and bring to the boil. Reduce heat to low and simmer, covered, for 12 minutes or until liquid is absorbed and quinoa is tender. Cool. Add quinoa to the thermo bowl with remaining ingredients.

  15 seconds

  4

Blend until nice and smooth.

Chicken & Apple Fingers

Makes 16

- 250g chicken, breast or thigh, roughly chopped
- 1 apple, cored and chopped
- 1 carrot, chopped
- ½ garlic clove
- ½ small brown onion, chopped
- 1 egg yolk
- ¼ cup (15g) freshly grated wholemeal breadcrumbs
- ½ teaspoon fresh thyme leaves

Place the chicken into the thermo bowl.

 10 seconds

 7

Remove and set aside. Add the apple, carrot, garlic and onion.

 4 seconds

Add remaining three ingredients and the chicken mince.

 30 seconds

 3

Take small balls of mixture and roll into little 'fingers.' Place on a paper-lined baking tray and grill for 8 minutes on each side. Allow to cool before serving to the pleasure of your baby.

TIP: For best results when mincing your own meat, partially frozen meat is easiest to mince.

Chicken & Apple Purée

Makes 2 to 3 serves

- ½ a small onion, peeled and chopped
- 1 tablespoon (15g) butter
- 100g chicken breast, cut into small pieces
- 1 carrot, peeled and chopped
- 300g sweet potato, peeled and chopped
- 1 Granny Smith (100g) apple, peeled and chopped
- ¾ cup (190g) unsalted chicken stock

Into the thermo bowl, place onion.

 5 seconds

 5

Scrape down the sides and add the butter.

 4 minutes

 100°C

 2

Add the chicken.

 3 minutes

 100°C

 2

Add everything else.

 12 minutes

 100°C

 6

Cool slightly then purée to your desired consistency.

Coconut Quinoa Pudding

Makes 2 cups

- ½ cup (100g) quinoa
- 400g can coconut milk
- 2 tablespoons (30g) agave syrup (or honey)

Place quinoa in a fine sieve and rinse under cold running water. Drain well. Place quinoa, coconut milk and agave nectar into the thermo bowl.

 14 minutes

 80°C

 1

Set aside for 5 minutes to cool. The quinoa will continue to absorb the coconut milk and thicken a little until ready to eat.

OPTIONAL: Serve warm with fresh or stewed fruits.

Country Casserole

Makes 2 cups

- 1 teaspoon vegetable oil
- ⅓ cup (30g) washed and chopped white part of leek
- 1 chicken thigh, skinned and trimmed of fat
- 2 medium carrots, peeled and chopped
- 1 cup (250g) unsalted chicken stock
- ¼ cup (30g) frozen peas

Place the leek and oil into the thermo bowl.

 4 minutes

 80°C

 1

Add the chicken.

 4 minutes

 80°C

 1

Add the carrots and pour in the stock.

 15 minutes

 90°C

 1

With 5 minutes to go, remove the MC, add the peas and continue cooking. Cool for 5 minutes.

 10 seconds

 8

Fruity Teething Treats

Makes 2 cups

- 8 strawberries, washed and hulled
- 300g watermelon, diced
- 2 apples, cored and sliced
- ½ mango, peeled and cubed

Place all ingredients into the thermo bowl.

  5 seconds

Pour the mixture into popsicle moulds and freeze for at least 4 hours or until set.

Lamb Hot Pot

Makes 2 cups

- ½ an onion, peeled and sliced in two
- 1 carrot, chopped
- 275g sweet potato, peeled and chopped
- 100g lean lamb, chopped
- 1 cup (250g) vegetable stock

Place the onion, carrot and sweet potato into the thermo bowl.

 5 seconds

 8

Add the lamb.

 4 minutes

 90°C

 1

Add the stock.

 10 minutes

 90°C

 4

Use turbo boost to purée if not to your desired consistency. Allow soup to cool before blending using the Turbo Boost Function until desired consistency is achieved.

Mango & Chia Seed Pudding

Serves 2

- 1 large mango
- 1 tablespoon (10g) chia seeds

Remove the flesh from the mango, discarding the skin and seed and place into the thermo bowl.

 15 seconds

 7

Add chia seeds.

 5 seconds

 4

Pour into a bowl and refrigerate for 15 minutes or until the pudding sets.

OPTIONAL: Add the flesh of a mango with ¾ cup of ice cubes to the thermo bowl. Turbo boost for 5 seconds or until a deliciously creamy **Mango Sorbet** *results.*

Mushroom & Bread Puree

Makes 1½ cups

- 1 cup (250g) **Cream of Mushroom Soup** (see p. 133)
- 1 slice wholemeal bread, crusts removed

Place ingredients into the thermo bowl.

 2 minutes

 70°C

 8

Peach Lassi Ice-blocks

Makes 26

- 1 cup (250g) vanilla yoghurt
- 1 tablespoon honey
- 1 teaspoon ground cardamom
- 400g can peach slices in juice, drained

Place all the ingredients into the thermo bowl.

 20 seconds

 8

Pour the mixture into ice cream moulds. Tap moulds gently on the bench. Insert sticks. Lock into place and freeze over night or until firm.

Poached Salmon with Garden Veggies

Makes 2 cups

- 30g cheddar cheese, cubed
- 1 potato, peeled and sliced
- 1 carrot, peeled and sliced
- ⅔ cup (165g) vegetable stock
- 120g salmon fillet, skinned and chopped
- 2 tablespoons (30g) peas

Place the cheese into the thermo bowl.

 4 seconds

 8

Remove and set aside. Add potato, carrot and stock.

 8 minutes

 80°C

 1

Add the salmon.

 4 minutes

 80°C

 1

With 2 minutes remaining, remove the MC and add the peas and cheese. Check consistency and blend for 4 seconds / speed 8 if not yet pureed.

Zucchini Slice

Makes 20 squares

- 1 carrot, roughly chopped
- 1 parsnip, roughly chopped
- 2 zucchini, roughly chopped
- 100g baby spinach leaves
- 2 tablespoons (30g) olive oil
- 1 tablespoon finely chopped chives (or parsley)
- 2 tablespoons plain flour
- 5 whole eggs
- ¾ cup (75g) grated cheddar cheese

Preheat oven to 180°C. Add carrot, parsnip, zucchini and spinach to the thermo bowl.

 10 seconds

 7

Add olive oil.

 5 minutes

 100°C

 1

Meanwhile, line a 28 x 18cm slice tin (or 18cm square cake tin for a thicker slice) with baking paper. Add remaining ingredients to the thermo bowl.

 10 seconds

 1

Scrape down the sides of the bowl and repeat until just incorporated. Pour the mixture into the slice tin and bake for 20 minutes or until lightly golden. Allow to cool in the tin, then remove and slice into small squares for your toddler.

Index

Dips

Breads & Doughs

Lunches

SALADS

DRESSINGS, MARINADES & SAUCES

ALL OTHERS

Mains 130

SOUPS

CHICKEN, MEAT & SEAFOOD

RISOTTOS

VEGETARIAN

SIDES

Invitation
to join our THERMO-STRUCK family

Our wish is to cultivate a family of foodies all bound together
by the desire to create good, healthy, homemade meals quickly,
easily and economically.

Our aim is to save us all precious time and money in the kitchen.
If this is you too, then we invite you to join our growing family where
we share kitchen wisdom daily.

facebook.com/4ingredientspage

@4ingredients

4 Ingredients Channel

4ingredients.com.au

@4ingredients

@4ingredients

Wishing you Thermost amazing experience

Kim